About This Book

Why is this topic importar.

For highest retention of new knowledge or skills, learners must be actively involved in their own learning. Activities used in training, workshops, classrooms, and groups should meet the specific needs of participants for connecting with others, interacting with new information, addressing difficult issues, and working together. Most important, perhaps, the intent of the activity must fit with the goals of the training. Training and workshops that do not incorporate activities to engage participants are, in essence, lectures. This book not only offers a great variety of new and exciting activities, but also simplifies the process of incorporating appropriate activities into training and group work.

What can you achieve with this book?

This book offers trainers and group leaders the tools to create lively and interactive training sessions and group work. You can choose from a large variety of activities that will move participants through getting acquainted, building teams, addressing issues, developing effective working relationships, and learning and retaining new information. The Adjourning section offers activities to bring closure to the training and to transition participants back to the workplace.

How is this book organized?

The book is divided into five sections, with sections within sections based on the types of activities. The format of the book is designed to reflect the process of group development and is a framework for the organization of the activities. The introduction to each section includes explanations for the use of particular activities and an abundance of training tips for working with groups. The accompanying CD-ROM contains copies of all the handouts and worksheets.

About Pfeiffer

Pfeiffer serves the professional development and hands-on resource needs of training and human resource practitioners and gives them products to do their jobs better. We deliver proven ideas and solutions from experts in HR development and HR management, and we offer effective and customizable tools to improve workplace performance. From novice to seasoned professional, Pfeiffer is the source you can trust to make yourself and your organization more successful.

Essential Knowledge   Pfeiffer produces insightful, practical, and comprehensive materials on topics that matter the most to training and HR professionals. Our Essential Knowledge resources translate the expertise of seasoned professionals into practical, how-to guidance on critical workplace issues and problems. These resources are supported by case studies, worksheets, and job aids and are frequently supplemented with CD-ROMs, Web sites, and other means of making the content easier to read, understand, and use.

Essential Tools   Pfeiffer's Essential Tools resources save time and expense by offering proven, ready-to-use materials—including exercises, activities, games, instruments, and assessments—for use during a training or team-learning event. These resources are frequently offered in looseleaf or CD-ROM format to facilitate copying and customization of the material.

Pfeiffer also recognizes the remarkable power of new technologies in expanding the reach and effectiveness of training. While e-hype has often created whizbang solutions in search of a problem, we are dedicated to bringing convenience and enhancements to proven training solutions. All our e-tools comply with rigorous functionality standards. The most appropriate technology wrapped around essential content yields the perfect solution for today's on-the-go trainers and human resource professionals.

www.pfeiffer.com

Essential resources for training and HR professionals

Miriam McLaughlin
Sandra Peyser

The NEW
Encyclopedia
of
ICEBREAKERS

Pfeiffer
A Wiley Imprint
www.pfeiffer.com

Acquiring Editor: *Martin Delahoussaye*
Director of Development: *Kathleen Dolan Davies*
Developmental Editor: *Susan Rachmeler*
Production Editor: *Nina Kreiden*
Editor: *Rebecca Taff*
Editorial Assistant: *Laura Reizman*
Manufacturing Supervisor: *Bill Matherly*

Interior Design: *Gene Crofts*
Cover Design: *Chris Wallace*
Illustrations: *ICC*

HB Printing 10 9 8 7 6 5
PB Printing 10 9 8 7 6 5 4 3 2 1

➤ Contents

Section 2: Storming   83

Section 3: Norming 145

Section 4: Performing   217

➤ Introduction: Getting the Most from This Resource

Purpose

This book is designed to help organizations train personnel in new skills and information effectively and efficiently. Facilitators, trainers, group leaders, and teachers will find this book to be a comprehensive resource for the work they do in training rooms, at meetings, and in the classroom.

In spite of the title, most of the activities in this book go beyond simple icebreakers. The Storming section, for example, offers activities that explore diversity, conflict, and communication. The intent here is to offer a broad variety of activities from which trainers and facilitators can choose.

The need for effective and efficient training has never been greater. There is a constant flow of new information and a constant demand for new skills. Time constraints and costs, however, require that training be focused, organized, and meaningful. This book provides a comprehensive guide to trainers to ensure they are prepared to meet requirements of the training as well as the needs of participants.

Audience

The New Encyclopedia of Icebreakers has been written for people who work with groups. Whether experienced or novice, trainers, teachers, group leaders, and facilitators are among the professionals who will find this book invaluable. The activities have been tested in training sessions and with groups and teams and have proven effective in these various settings. Many of these activities are appropriate for use with young people in school or college settings.

How This Resource Is Organized

The New Encyclopedia of Icebreakers is divided into five sections, with sections within sections based on the types of activities. The sections follow the stages of group development. This format is intended as a guide to choosing activities appropriate for a particular group or training. For example, a two- or three-hour training would have an introductory activity or icebreaker (found in the Forming section) and, perhaps, an activity for interacting with the information presented in the training (Performing section). A longer training session, or an ongoing team or group, in contrast, would be more likely to use communication and conflict activities (Storming section) and team-building activities (Norming section). All training and group sessions should have some opportunity for closure, and appropriate activities for this purpose are found in the Adjourning section. The trainer or facilitator must consider the objectives of the training or group work, the time the group will be together, and the demographics of the audience when selecting activities.

At the beginning of each section, an introduction describes ways to use the activities in the section and tips for trainers and group leaders.

The first section, Forming, offers get-acquainted and grouping activities. These activities are necessary to the beginning of any form of group work. The second section, Storming, focuses on the issues that arise in work and academic environments as people struggle to learn to work together. Communication, diversity, and conflict resolution are among the subjects of the activities in this section. Section 3, Norming, has activities that help people build teams and practice working effectively together. The subject matter and material from the training can be incorporated into the fourth section, Performing. Activities in this section give participants the opportunity to interact with and reflect on information from the training. Finally, closure activities make up the fifth section, entitled Adjourning.

At the conclusion of each activity is a section entitled "Trainer/ Facilitator Insights," which provides space for the trainer to make notes. Things such as what worked well and what did not for a particular group, participant questions, and ideas for using the activity again can all be noted in this section for future reference.

In addition, the accompanying CD includes copies of all the hand-outs and worksheets.

The Stages of Group Development

This book is designed to align with the stages of group development, based on Tuckman's model.* The stages are indicative of the process individuals go through as they attempt to form a working team.

In the *forming* stage, people are generally polite and guardedly friendly. They need help to begin developing relationships with others in the group. This book offers that help in the form of get-acquainted and grouping activities that encourage interaction among group members. As they begin building relationships, their comfort levels increase, and these individuals are better prepared for interactive learning experiences.

The second stage of group development is *storming,* when individuals begin to assert themselves and resist the formation of the group. Poor communication, diverse interests, and conflicts are all issues during this stage. The *Storming* section of the book offers numerous activities to help groups work through this difficult stage. Groups seldom accomplish much actual work during this time, but do work through the obstacles to effective performance as teams.

Norming is the settling-in stage, when people begin to identify themselves as a group or team. They start to practice teamwork and agree to common goals. The activities in this section offer opportunities for practicing teamwork. Activities are also included to help energize participants as they continue their work.

The fourth stage of group development is *performing.* At this point, the group is highly productive. Groups are able to make joint decisions and diagnose and solve problems. In this fourth section, activities are provided that allow participants to interact with the information they are learning in the training.

We have included another section for a stage that is not always included in models of group development. The *Adjourning* section offers activities that allow groups to reach closure and transition back to the

*Tuckman, B. (1965). Developmental Sequence in Small Groups. *Psychological Bulletin, 63,* 384–399.

workplace. The longer people are together, the greater their need to bring closure to their work as a group. This section offers some closures that are brief and simple and others that are more extensive. Activities are also offered that allow participants to consider how they will apply their new learning back on the job.

Selection Guidelines

There are a number of considerations when choosing activities for your training or group work, such as:

- Who are the participants? Are they part of the same workplace or organization or coming from a variety of places? Do they know each other or are they strangers? Are they educators, technical workers, college students, or businesspeople?

- How many participants are there going to be?

- How long will the participants be working together? Are they part of an ongoing team or a one-day training?

- What is the subject or focus of the training or group work?

- How much time is allotted for the work of the training or group?

- What do you want the activities to accomplish?

- What training materials are needed? Do you have access to them?

The activities in this book are formatted to give the trainer/facilitator all the information necessary to select the activities appropriate for the planned training or group work. The purpose of each activity is stated under the title. Also included is the time the activity will take, numbers of participants who can effectively do the activity, and the materials and preparation required. The stated times are based on the suggested number of participants for the activities. The larger the number of participants, the longer the activity will take. Also included in the times is the assumption that you will be taking a few minutes to give instructions to participants.

Levels of Risk

Risk level refers to what activities require of participants and their readiness to do what is required. When selecting activities, consider the relationships that exist among participants. If they are complete strangers, choose introductory activities that require limited personal sharing (*low risk*). Participants will feel safe talking about their jobs, families, and hobbies. At this level, physical contact between participants should not exceed a handshake.

For groups from the same workplace, where at least surface relationships exist, the trainer/facilitator can go a step further, using introductory activities that ask participants to reveal some things about themselves (*moderate risk*). This level of relationship in the group allows for some physical touching, for example, a pat on the back. Moderate-risk activities can also be used with groups that have had enough time together to build a friendly rapport. Trainers and facilitators can use these activities to challenge participants to move to the next level of sharing.

Using *high-risk* activities requires a trust level among participants that allows them to reveal feelings, share ideas and knowledge, or be involved in physical activities requiring touch. Arm linking, back-to-back partnering, and even hugging can occur once participants feel safe and accepted in the group. Trainers and facilitators should use these activities to promote maximum learning and involvement in the training or group.

The activities in *The New Encyclopedia of Icebreakers* offer all the levels of risk and are accompanied by clear descriptions that will guide trainers and facilitators in making the appropriate choices.

➤ Section 1

Forming

The Forming section offers activities for mixing and grouping participants and involving them in introductions and interactions with others. These activities prepare participants for involvement in the training that follows.

The Forming stage of group development refers to that time when people first come together to attend a training session, develop a team, or begin a group. There are patterns of behavior at this stage that are typical, whether the participants are present for training, forming a group, or working with a team.

People come into new situations as individuals, with unique ideas of what to expect from the experience. Some may be fearful, others impatient, and still others resistant or intrigued. Some may have been required by a supervisor to attend and others may have enrolled voluntarily. The reasons people are in attendance often affect their initial attitudes.

For example, one training held by a small corporation required attendance by all corporate staff. It seems the CEO of the company had discovered a new way of improving linkage between departments and wanted to implement the method companywide. Response from the staff ranged from strong resistance to the idea to acceptance of the inevitable. Many staff members held a "show me" attitude. The trainer in this case had to help the participants move beyond these expectations. He did so by mixing people up into small groups to separate and defuse the negative attitudes. He then used a get-acquainted activity to get the group members talking and eventually to move them toward personal sharing. His careful approach produced a more cooperative and positive response from participants to the actual "meat" of the training.

For the most part, however, participants are polite and cooperative at the forming stage. Trainers, facilitators, and team leaders can take advantage of this attitude of cooperation by gently encouraging the participants to get to know each other, to talk, and to share. As people begin to communicate with others, they begin to move toward involvement with the work of the group. Until participants have an opportunity to speak, they will not join the work of the training or team.

Selecting Activities

Activities used at the beginning of training sessions or meetings should be low risk. People aren't in a place where they are comfortable calling attention to themselves, standing and speaking alone, or revealing personal information. To maintain this low level of risk, the activities in this section invite participants to share in groups or with partners and to offer only as much information about themselves, their thoughts, or feelings as they feel comfortable sharing.

Choose activities according to the personality characteristics of the group or team with whom you will be working. People who are logical, rational thinkers, for example, will be more task oriented (focused on the work and outcomes) than people who are more relationship oriented and will be concerned with process (looking at how the group does the work). Providing a variety of activities for diverse groups helps ensure the involvement of all participants.

Also, the length of the training or length of time a team or group will be together is very important in choosing introductory activities. For shorter training sessions, use short activities that may only require sharing names and a little personal history. The longer the group is going to be together, the more time should be devoted to getting acquainted.

When you, as facilitator or trainer, find yourself feeling awkward or uncomfortable leading an activity, do something different. You are a model for how participants will respond to any activity, so choose something that you enjoy doing.

Why Group Participants?

Breaking up a large group of people into small working groups allows all participants to be involved in the activities and sharing that are part of interactive training. Participants feel safer, less exposed, and are more likely to share information and ideas with small groups of people. In addition, grouping reduces the time required for any activity. For example, if fifty people take turns introducing themselves, it could take an hour or more to hear from everyone. Giving participants the opportunity to introduce themselves in small groups will take just a few minutes.

We recommend that all groups of more than eight or ten participants always be grouped. Grouping helps move the training along and provides opportunities for greater participation. The trainer can have small groups cover material in ways that allow everyone to interact with the material and information in the training. Participants working in small groups have more opportunities to speak than those in one large group do. Small groups usually develop a level of trust as the work proceeds that allows for open sharing of thoughts and ideas.

It is important to mix people up before forming groups or teams to improve participants' opportunities to connect with new and different people. Most people will, if given the choice, sit with people they know. There are also the occasional hostile pockets of participants who were coerced into attendance and who are influenced by each other's negative feelings. Separating these people defuses the hostility and encourages their buy-in as the training progresses. Using a game to mix people up and to form teams is an efficient approach and reduces resistance from participants who don't want to leave their chosen space.

Once groups are formed, participants will need to begin connecting with other group members. Again, get-acquainted activities accomplish this task in nonthreatening ways. While the activities suggest that participating in sharing is required, participants have the freedom to choose how much or how little they say.

Common Issues in Training and Group Work

What if . . .

- *The participants already know one another?* It is still important for participants to have an opportunity to meet and greet one another. No one is part of a group until he or she speaks in the group. It is equally important that participants be mixed up before grouping, as they will still be sitting with their closest acquaintances.

- *A participant absolutely refuses to move?* At the end of the grouping activity, simply ask a group to join that person. Under no circumstances should you try to force that person to participate. There are people who have severe phobias about new situations.

- *People come in after the introductory activity has begun?* Lead those people to a group and ask that all group members reintroduce themselves. Explain the rest of the activity to the newcomer.

- *The training or meeting room is not set up for group work?* Improvise. If you are stuck with theater style, put groups in two rows, half the group sitting in front of the other half. They can then turn around for discussions and activities.

- *Your training or meeting room is a large conference room?* Move the chairs and tables needed for the number of participants you are expecting to one side of the room and turn over the chairs that you do not want participants to use. Also, large conference rooms are infamous for being too hot or too cold. Encourage people to let you know if they are uncomfortable, and assure them you will do what you can to fix the problem.

- *Your training or meeting room is really too small for your group?* Prior to starting the training, identify additional space where groups can work. Hallways, offices, and other meeting rooms can serve as workspace for small groups. Do a minimal amount of lecture with the whole group, and then give assignments and move from group to group to teach other concepts.

- *The numbers of participants exceeds fifty?* When you have over fifty participants in a training, time is a major issue. Moving large numbers of people around is time-consuming. To help control time, plan assigned seating, prior to the training, that will mix participants up and put them in teams. Put colors or numbers that match with tables on nametags to indicate where participants will sit for the training. Also, with large groups, ask for volunteers to share results rather than having every team report out every time. Another concern with large groups is breaks. Getting people out of the room and back in takes time. We recommend that you have fewer and longer breaks and use the energizer activities found in Section 3 to allow people to take breaks from the work without leaving their seats.

- *There are fewer than ten participants?* When you have fewer than ten people show up for a training, the time problem is reversed. Everything, from introductions to activities, takes much less time. There is also less energy and enthusiasm to build on with a small group. Try to avoid this situation by requiring that a minimum number of participants be signed up in order to hold the training. If you end up working with a small number—anywhere from three to nine participants—give them roles in presenting parts of the material. They can use your planned activities or invent their own. This approach gives participants responsibility for their own learning and the learning of the others in the group. It engages participants and promotes involvement.

Planning Ahead

Dear Diary: Getting Started

Letter Writing

Shared Agreements

Tuck Away

➤ Dear Diary: Getting Started

Purpose   Trainers should use this activity for training lasting longer than a day. This activity is designed to give participants regular opportunities to reflect on new learning and experiences they have during the training.

Risk Level   Low

Time   10 minutes at the middle and end of each training day

Number of Participants   Twenty-five maximum

Materials/Preparation
- Small notebooks provided to participants are nice but not necessary.

Directions
1. Explain to participants that they will be keeping a diary of their training experiences.
2. They will be expected to reflect in writing on any new learning or experiences they have during the training.
3. Allow no more than 10 minutes before lunch and at the end of the day for participants to write in their diaries.

Processing the Activity
- Ask participants if they came up with questions during their reflection about the material covered to this point.
- Take time to address any questions. Let participants know that they will be sharing some of their thoughts and insights on the last day of the training. (*Note:* The closure for this activity is Dear Diary: Closure in the Adjourning section.)

Trainer/Facilitator Insights

_____

_____

_____

_____

_____

_____

_____

_____

➤ Letter Writing

Purpose   This activity gives trainers a formal way of welcoming participants and describing their expectations for the training.

Risk Level   Low

Time   15 minutes

Number of Participants   Unlimited

Materials/Preparation
- A copy of the letter (see sample) for each participant. The letter can be sent to participants in advance of the training.

Directions
1. Write a letter to participants based on the sample provided, and make a copy for each participant. You may want to address specifics of the topic of the training or group work in the letter.
2. Distribute the letters as participants arrive at the training or mail in advance of the training.
3. Review the letter with participants prior to starting the training and ask if there are any questions.

Processing the Activity
- See Letter Writing Continued in the Adjourning section.

Trainer/Facilitator Insights

_____

_____

_____

_____

_____

_____

_____

_____

Letter Writing: Letter to Participants

Dear participants in the_____training (group):

I want to welcome you as a participant in the_____. Our work begins at_____o'clock and ends at_____o'clock each day [today]. I will start and end the training on time. Please make every effort to be here on time and to stay for the entire training. Also, please keep to the allotted times for lunch and breaks.

   We will be working hard during our time together, and I look forward to your full participation. It is my hope that you will be challenged and have fun during this training session and that it will be a rewarding learning experience for all of us.

Sincerely,
[NAME]
[CREDENTIALS]

⯈ Shared Agreements

Purpose   This activity establishes the expectations of the trainer and the participants at the start of the training.

Risk Level   Low

Time   15 minutes

Number of Participants   Unlimited

Materials/Preparation
- Flip chart
- Markers

Directions
1. Explain to participants that at the beginning of the training it is a good idea for the trainer and the trainees (or group) to come to some shared agreements about expectations for the training.
2. Give an example: "One of my expectations is that everyone here will participate. One of your expectations may be that we end on time."
3. With the group, brainstorm expectations (yours and theirs) and write them on flip chart paper. Allow 10 minutes for this part of the activity.
4. Keep the shared agreements visible throughout the training.

Processing the Activity
- Ask participants why it is important for the trainer and participant to have shared agreements (reduces misunderstandings during the training).

Trainer/Facilitator Insights

_____

_____

_____

_____

_____

_____

_____

_____

➤ Tuck Away

Purpose   This activity encourages participants to make the transition from their work and personal life to the training.

Risk Level   Low

Time   10 minutes

Number of Participants   Unlimited

Materials/Preparation
- Plain paper and an envelope for each participant

Directions
1. Instruct participants to write their names on the backs of their envelopes.
2. Tell them to write down all the cares, worries, and responsibilities they left behind when they came to the training on a piece of paper and place it in the envelope. Allow 5 minutes for this part of the activity.
3. Collect the envelopes and tell them that their cares, worries, and responsibilities are now tucked away and their minds are free to focus on new learning.

Processing the Activity
- Tell participants they will revisit what they wrote at the end of the training. (See Tuck Away II in the Adjourning section.)

Trainer/Facilitator Insights

_____

_____

_____

_____

_____

_____

_____

_____

_____

Forming Groups

The Continents

It's a Puzzle

Quotables

Snapshots

Synonyms

True Colors

➤ The Continents

Purpose   This activity mixes participants up and puts them in groups.

Risk Level   Low

Time   25 minutes

Number of Participants   Forty-eight maximum

Materials/Preparation
- Masking tape
- Six pieces of flip chart paper, with a continent written on each one
- Index cards, each with a different country, city, province, or state written on it, one per participant

  Note: Use the Continents, Countries, Provinces, States, and Cities list that follows the activity to assist in preparing the flip chart sheets and index cards. For smaller groups, just remove index cards evenly from different continents.

Directions
1. Using masking tape, post the flip chart papers in various areas of the room.
2. Distribute index cards, one per participant.
3. Tell participants that they have the name of a country, city, province, or state found on one of the six continents.
4. Instruct them to go and stand under the continent where they believe their country, city, province, or state is located. Tell them they can help each other. Allow 10 minutes for this part of the activity, although most groups finish before time is up.

5. Once they are in their continent groups, ask them to introduce themselves and share a travel experience. Allow 10 minutes for this part of the activity.

6. Instruct the groups to move their things and sit together.

Processing the Activity

- Ask participants what the activity accomplished. (It mixed them up and put them in groups.)
- Ask if anyone got a country, city, province, or state he or she would like to visit and why.

Trainer/Facilitator Insights

_____

_____

_____

_____

_____

_____

_____

_____

The Continents, Countries, States, Provinces, and Cities

Africa	South America	Asia
Egypt	Brazil	China
Kenya	Argentina	India
Algeria	Bolivia	Pakistan
Morocco	Uruguay	Russia
Mozambique	Paraguay	South Korea
Tanzania	Chile	Turkey
Mali	Venezuela	Saudi Arabia
Ethiopia	Ecuador	Thailand

North America	Europe	Australia
Mexico	Norway	New South Wales
Alberta	France	Melbourne
Ontario	Spain	Sydney
Quebec	Portugal	Brisbane
California	England	Perth
New York	Switzerland	Canberra
Alaska	Germany	Queensland
Florida	Romania	Adelaide

➤ It's a Puzzle

Purpose   This activity is designed to form small, mixed groups.

Risk Level   Low

Time   15 minutes

Number of Participants   Forty maximum

Materials/Preparation
- Poster paper, one piece for each question. Poster paper should all be the same color.
- Write the questions from the Questions for the Puzzles sheet (or use your own) in large print on individual pieces of poster paper or cardboard. Prepare as many pieces of poster paper as you want groups for the training.
- *Cut the posters in the same number of pieces as you want people in your groups.* For example, if you want six people per group, cut each puzzle into six pieces. The pieces should be cut jigsaw style. Once you have all the posters cut into pieces, mix the pieces up.

Directions
1. Give each participant a puzzle piece as he/she arrives at the training session.
2. Tell people that they must find the other people with pieces to their puzzle before the training starts.
3. They should sit with this group of people and discuss their question.

Processing the Activity
- Welcome participants.
- Be sure each group has had an opportunity to answer the question on their puzzle.
- Ask for volunteers to share something they learned about a group member.

Trainer/Facilitator Insights

_____

_____

_____

_____

_____

_____

_____

_____

It's a Puzzle: Questions for the Puzzles

What is your favorite vacation spot?

What do you do when you are not working?

Who are the most significant people in your life and why?

Where would you live if you could live anywhere?

What is your favorite book or movie and why?

What is your prize possession?

What historical figure would you invite to dinner?

Note: Instead of using the questions above, you could write questions or statements related to the training on the puzzles.

➤ Quotables

Purpose   This activity helps participants to mix with others and find a partner.

Risk Level   Low to Moderate

Time   20 minutes

Number of Participants   Twenty-six (more can be accommodated if trainer increases the number of quotes)

Materials/Preparation
- Thirteen index cards with quotes written on them (see the Quotables: Quotes and Speakers list)
- Thirteen index cards with the quoted person's name on them

Directions
1. Shuffle the cards and give one to each participant.
2. Tell participants to find their partners by matching the quote and the person who said it. Because some people may not recognize certain quotes, it is important that participants help each other make the matches (10 minutes).
3. Once they have made their matches, tell them to move their things and sit with their partners.
4. Ask them to interview one another in preparation for introducing their partners to the larger group.
5. Have each pair stand and introduce each other.

Processing the Activity
- Ask what this activity accomplished. (It mixed people up and moved them around.)
- Ask participants what they learned.

Trainer/Facilitator Insights

_____

_____

_____

_____

_____

_____

_____

_____

Quotables: Quotes and Speakers List

That's one small step for man, one giant leap forward for mankind.

Float like a butterfly, sting like a bee.

When in doubt, tell the truth.

The physician can bury his mistakes, but the architect can only advise his clients to plant vines.

Why don't you come up and see me sometime?

Father, I cannot tell a lie, I did it with my little hatchet.

In the future, everybody will be world famous for fifteen minutes.

Love conquers all things.

A lie gets halfway around the world before the truth has a chance to get its pants on.

And so, my fellow Americans, ask not what your country can do for you. Ask what you can do for your country.

I have a dream . . .

Sir, I have not yet begun to fight.

If at first you don't succeed, try, try again.

Neil Armstrong

Muhammad Ali

Mark Twain

Frank Lloyd Wright

Mae West

George Washington

Andy Warhol

Virgil

Sir Winston Churchill

John F. Kennedy

Martin Luther King

John Paul Jones

William Hickson

Source: Jones, A., with Pickering, S., & Thomson, M. (Eds.). (1996). *Chambers Dictionary of Quotations.* Edinburgh: Chambers, an imprint of Larousse ple.

➤ Snapshots

Purpose This activity helps participants find partners and get acquainted.

Risk Level Low

Time 20 minutes

Number of Participants Twenty maximum

Materials/Preparation
- Polaroid™ camera
- Extra film
- Flip chart paper
- Tape or glue
- Markers

   Note: A participant who arrives early can be asked to help you with this preparation.

Directions
1. Take a Polaroid picture of each participant as he or she arrives.
2. Spread the pictures on a table at the front of the room and pair them up.
3. Invite participants up to the table to find their own picture and meet their partner (5 minutes).
4. Give each set of partners a piece of flip chart paper, tape or glue, and markers.
5. Ask them to glue their pictures to the paper.
6. Ask participants to talk with each other, and as they learn something about their partners, to write the information on the flip chart paper under the partner's picture (5 minutes).

7. At the completion of the activity, invite the partners to post their pictures on the wall.
8. Give everyone a chance to walk around and "meet" the other participants by reading their flip chart papers (10 minutes).

Processing the Activity

• Ask participants what they found intriguing about each other.
• Encourage participants to seek each other out during breaks in the training.

Trainer/Facilitator Insights

_____

_____

_____

_____

_____

_____

_____

_____

➤ Synonyms

Purpose   This activity is intended to form small, mixed groups.

Risk Level   Low

Time   30 minutes

Number of Participants   Thirty maximum

Materials/Preparation   Thirty slips of paper, each with a different word written on it, one word per piece of paper. (For a list of the words, see the Synonyms List at the end of this activity.)

Note: For groups with fewer than thirty people, remove slips from different groupings of words.

Directions
1. Mix the slips of paper together and distribute them, one to each participant.
2. Tell participants they are to find others who have synonyms (words that have the same, or nearly the same, meaning) for their words. Allow 5 minutes for this part of the activity.
3. Once they have found their synonym group, they should get their materials and sit with their group (5 minutes).
4. Tell participants to introduce themselves and share one thing they hope to gain from this workshop that is related to the synonyms in their group. For example, a participant in the skill/proficiency group might share the desire to gain proficiency in [subject of training] (15 minutes).

Processing the Activity

- Ask for a volunteer from each group to share what members of the group hoped to gain from the training related to their synonyms.
- Explain that this training will supply the information and the tools for participants to gain knowledge and skills in the area of [training subject].

Trainer/Facilitator Insights

_____

_____

_____

_____

_____

_____

_____

_____

Synonyms List

Information	Data	Facts	Statistics	Records	Figures
Tools	Gear	Equipment	Utensils	Apparatus	Paraphernalia
Plan	Strategy	Diagram	Map	Sketch	Graph
Knowledge	Wisdom	Insight	Perception	Astuteness	Acumen
Skill	Proficiency	Ability	Talent	Know-how	Competence

➤ True Colors

Purpose   This activity creates mixed groups and provides participants an opportunity to share.

Risk Level   Low

Time   20 minutes

Number of Participants   Unlimited (in small groups of six to eight)

Materials/Preparation
- Name tags
- A variety of colored dots. Stick dots on name tags using the dif-
  ferent colors to create groups. For example, if you want to create
  groups of eight, put green dots on eight of the name tags.
- Table signs with the different colors on them

  Note: For a large number of participants, you may want to use
  crayons to make the dots, as this will provide access to a greater
  number of colors.

Directions
1. Distribute name tags. As participants arrive, tell them to sit at the
   tables that display the same colors as the dots on their name
   tags.
2. Once participants are seated, ask them to introduce themselves
   to their groups and share a role that the table color plays in their
   lives. For example, someone seated at the red table may have a
   red car. Someone seated at the yellow table may enjoy being
   outside in the sunshine. Each person in the group should be
   allowed 3 minutes to share.

Processing the Activity

- Ask for volunteers to share something interesting they learned from other group members.
- Ask how colors affect our work environment and our lives.

Trainer/Facilitator Insights

_____

_____

_____

_____

_____

_____

_____

_____

Getting Acquainted

Collectible Items

For Sale

Forced Choices

Get Acquainted Quietly

Give a Sign

Head to Toe

In the News

It's in the Cards

Keep It Up

The Kid in All of Us

Pals

⊇ Collectible Items

Purpose   This activity is ideal for a one-day training session. It encourages participants to meet as many people as possible.

Risk Level   Low

Time   20 minutes

Number of Participants   Thirty maximum (in small groups of six to eight)

Materials/Preparation
- Small paper bags, one for each participant

Directions
1. Explain that participants will be trying to collect nonreturnable items from the other participants in the room. Distribute paper bags.

   Note: Collectible items may include business cards, gum, candy, paper clips, receipts—anything people are willing to give and not get back.

2. Tell them that they must first introduce themselves in their small groups and share one piece of personal information about themselves.

3. Once the groups have completed introductions, explain that they will have 5 minutes to move around the room introducing themselves to others. Participants introduce themselves to each person they meet and ask for a collectible item. Participants should respond to the askers by saying their names and either giving the askers items or saying they have nothing left to give away.

4. Explain that no one can take more than one item from any one person.

5. Once the participants have moved around the room attempting to collect from others for 5 minutes, ask them to return to their groups.

6. Tell participants to continue collecting items at breaks and lunch, never asking for an item from someone they have already met.

Processing the Activity

• See Collectible Items II in the Adjourning section.

Trainer/Facilitator Insights

_____

_____

_____

_____

_____

_____

_____

_____

➤ For Sale

Purpose   This activity is an energizing way for a small group of participants to learn each other's names.

Risk Level   Low to Moderate

Time   25 minutes

Number of Participants   Twenty maximum

Materials/Preparation
- Newspaper "For Sale" columns, each listing ten items, one column per participant

  Note: Choose a variety of For Sale columns, such as Furniture, Computers, Antiques, Boats, Livestock, Exercise Equipment, and Automobiles.

- A piece of plain paper for each participant
- Scissors for each participant
- A small envelope for each participant
- Glue sticks or tape for each participant

Directions
1. Distribute the columns, paper, scissors, small envelopes, and glue.
2. Tell participants to cut their For Sale columns into individual ads and place them in the envelopes.
3. Explain that they will be exchanging their items for items they want. They can only have one of a kind. If they have a column of cars for sale, for example, they can keep one, but must trade the rest for other things.
4. Tell them to introduce themselves and shake hands with participants before they try to trade. Allow 10 minutes for this part of the activity.

5. Once they have traded all their items, they should return to their seats and glue their new items to a plain piece of paper (5 minutes).
6. Instruct participants to find partners and explain to their partners why they chose the items they did. Allow 2 minutes for each partner to share.
7. Invite participants to write their names on their papers and post them around the room.

Processing the Activity

- Ask participants what they found interesting about other participants as a result of this activity.
- Ask participants if they learned anything about themselves from the items they chose to collect.

Trainer/Facilitator Insights

_____

_____

_____

_____

_____

_____

_____

_____

➤ Forced Choices

Purpose   This activity helps participants to identify things they have in common.

Risk Level   Low

Time   15 to 20 minutes

Number of Participants   Unlimited

Materials/Preparation
- Three pieces of paper numbered 1, 2, and 3 posted in different areas of the room
- A copy of the Forced Choice Statements sheet for the facilitator
- Masking tape

Directions
1. Tell participants that you will be reading statements and will offer three choices for completing the statements.
2. Point to three different parts of the room to which participants will move depending on their choices.
3. Read the first statement and the three choices from the Forced Choice Statements sheet. As you mention each choice, point to the different parts of the room.
4. Once everyone has made a choice, ask participants to introduce themselves in that group and tell why they made the choice they did. Allow the groups 3 minutes to share each time.
5. Repeat the above instructions with two more forced choice statements.

Processing the Activity
- Ask whether anyone met some of the same people each time.
- Note that people often have more in common than they realize.

Trainer/Facilitator Insights

_____

_____

_____

_____

_____

_____

_____

_____

Forced Choices: Forced Choice Statements

My favorite form of technology is . . . a cell phone, laptop, or PDA.

My favorite ethnic restaurant is . . . Mexican, Greek, or Italian.

My favorite form of transportation is . . . train, car, or plane.

⊒ Get Acquainted Quietly

Purpose   This activity offers participants an entertaining way to get to know one another.

Risk Level   Low to Moderate

Time   20 minutes

Number of Participants   Unlimited

Materials/Preparation   None

Directions
1. Tell participants that they are about to get to know someone else in this training session without speaking.
2. Instruct participants to silently look around the room and choose a partner through eye contact.
3. Tell them to go and stand next to their partners without speaking.
4. Explain that each partner will have 3 minutes to communicate information about himself or herself without speaking. Give an example: "Point to your wedding ring to indicate that you are married."
5. Tell participants you will call time at the end of 3 minutes and then the other partner will have 3 minutes to share silently.
6. At the end of the silent sharing, ask partners to tell each other what they learned from their silent conversation.

Processing the Activity
- Ask for volunteers to share how accurate or inaccurate they were in interpreting their partners' sharing.

- Ask the group whether they shared more or less than they would have verbally and why this was true.

Trainer/Facilitator Insights

_____

_____

_____

_____

_____

_____

_____

_____

⊠ Give a Sign

Purpose   This activity allows partners a unique way of introducing each other.

Risk Level   Low

Time   30 minutes

Number of Participants   Thirty maximum

Materials/Preparation
- Poster board cut in half (12 × 18), one half per participant
- Markers
- Masking tape

Directions
1. Ask participants to move around the room and partner up with someone they do not know.
2. Tell partners to introduce themselves and tell each other a few things about themselves. Explain that the information will be posted later and shared with the whole group. Each partner should have about 4 minutes to share.
3. Hand out the materials and instruct participants to design catchy billboards that advertise their partners, based on what their partners have shared (10 minutes).
4. Instruct each participant to introduce his or her partner to the group using the billboards they have designed.

Processing the Activity
- Ask participants to put their partners' names on the billboards and post them around the room.
- Invite participants to visit the billboards and learn about fellow participants during breaks from the training.

Trainer/Facilitator Insights

_____

_____

_____

_____

_____

_____

_____

_____

⊁ Head to Toe

Purpose   This activity uses the appearance of participants to "break the ice."

Risk Level   Moderate

Time   15 minutes

Number of Participants   Unlimited

Materials/Preparation
- A piece of flip chart paper with the following words listed on it: Head, Face, Shoulders, Arms, Hands, Torso, Legs, Feet
- Masking tape

Directions
1. Post the flip chart paper and instruct participants to stand and find partners.
2. Tell them to start with their heads and share something about themselves related to their heads. For example, a participant may have red hair she inherited from her Irish father.
3. Partners should then move to their faces, sharing something about their faces.
4. Instruct the participants to move through the posted list, sharing something about each listed part of their anatomy or about the clothing or accessories they are wearing. They can share their favorite use of their hands, what they enjoy putting in their stomachs, where they like their feet to take them, and so on.
5. After participants have been through the list for each of them, ask for volunteers to share something they learned about a partner.

Processing the Activity

- Ask how this activity helped participants get to know their partners.
- Ask why personal sharing is sometimes easier in a structured activity.

Trainer/Facilitator Insights

_____

_____

_____

_____

_____

_____

_____

_____

➤ In the News

Purpose   This activity is designed as a low-risk way to start participants talking with one another.

Risk Level   Low

Time   15 minutes

Number of Participants   Unlimited

Materials/Preparation
- Name tags numbered to indicate table assignments
- A numbered tent card for each table
- Headlines or articles cut from current newspapers or magazines for each table (Avoid controversial features.)

Directions
1. As participants arrive, instruct them to go to the tables that display the numbers on their name tags.
2. Welcome them as a whole group and ask them to introduce themselves to the other people at their tables.
3. Instruct table groups to spend about 8 minutes discussing the headlines or articles on their tables.

Processing the Activity
- Explain that most people have opinions or feelings about the events going on in the world.
- Ask for volunteers to share what their groups discussed.
- Ask participants what this activity accomplished.

Trainer/Facilitator Insights

_____

_____

_____

_____

_____

_____

_____

_____

➤ It's in the Cards

Purpose   This activity allows participants to make connections through playing cards.

Risk Level   Low to Moderate

Time   20 minutes

Number of Participants   Forty maximum (in small groups of six to eight)

Materials/Preparation
- One deck of playing cards per small group

Directions
1. Divide participants into small groups and give one person in each group a deck of playing cards. Instruct the participants with the card decks to deal three cards to each group member.
2. Explain that each participant is to make personal connections based on the numbers or symbols on his or her card. Give an example: "A Jack could represent the one you carry in the trunk of your new car. The Five of Hearts may represent members of your family. The Ace could represent some special skill you have."

   Note: Participants can be as silly or as serious as they wish in making personal connections to the cards.

3. Tell them to share those personal connections with their small groups. Each group member will just have 2 minutes to share.
4. Ask each small group to share with the entire group some of the most farfetched and the most informative connections group members made to their cards.

Processing the Activity

- Ask participants the purpose of using cards to instigate sharing. (The cards serve as triggers to help people share more and different things about themselves.)
- Ask how the shared information gives them a greater understanding of the group members.

Trainer/Facilitator Insights

_____

_____

_____

_____

_____

_____

_____

_____

_____

➤ Keep It Up

Purpose   This activity gives a small number of participants an energetic way to learn each other's names.

Risk Level   Low

Time   15 minutes

Number of Participants   Fifteen maximum

Materials/Preparation
- One large, inflated balloon and two additional inflated balloons for backup

Space Requirements   Open area that can accommodate a circle of participants

Directions
1. Instruct participants to stand in a large circle.
2. Tell them that they are going to start the balloon moving around the circle and they must keep it in the air and moving at all times.
3. Each time a participant has contact with the balloon, he or she must say his or her name.
4. Everyone should have contact with the balloon at least once. The balloon should move around the circle at least three times. If the balloon hits the floor, it must be returned to the person who first touched the balloon to begin again.
5. Start by throwing the balloon to someone in the circle.

Processing the Activity

- Ask for volunteers to tell the group whose names they remember.
- Ask how physical activity like the balloon game serves as an icebreaker.

Trainer/Facilitator Insights

_____

_____

_____

_____

_____

_____

_____

_____

⊒ The Kid in All of Us

Purpose   This activity allows participants to have a little fun introducing themselves to others.

Risk Level   Low to Moderate

Time   20 minutes

Number of Participants   Thirty (in small groups of five or six)

Materials/Preparation
- One balloon tied to the chair of each participant
- Toys placed in the middle of each group's table (blocks, small cars, puzzles, dolls, clay, crayons, and coloring books)

  Note: Many participants will play with the toys prior to the start of the workshop. If this occurs, note when you welcome them that there seems to be a lot of kid in us.

Directions
1. Ask participants to think about the kids they once were.
2. Ask them to share a little about their childhood with the rest of their group as a way of introducing themselves.
3. Tell them to share a little about what has changed in them as adults and what has not. Each group member will have 2 minutes to share.
4. Ask for volunteers to share what their group talked about.

Processing the Activity
- Note that the toy box is the child's workplace. Ask participants how it differs from the tools they use at work now.
- Invite participants to play with the toys during breaks in the training.

Trainer/Facilitator Insights

_____

_____

_____

_____

_____

_____

_____

_____

➤ Pals

Purpose   This activity allows participants to move around while becoming acquainted.

Risk Level   Low to Moderate

Time   15 minutes

Number of Participants   Unlimited

Materials/Preparation
- A CD player
- Music

Space Requirements   Open area, free of tables and chairs

Directions
1. Tell participants that when you play the music, they should move around the room smiling and nodding at one another.
2. When the music stops they are to find partners, shake hands, and introduce themselves. They should then find out where their partners were born. These people will always be their handshake partners.

   Note: Play the music for no more than 1 minute each time. Each time you stop the music, allow participants 3 minutes to talk with their new partners.

3. Next, tell participants that this time, when the music stops, they will partner up with new people, introduce themselves, and give their partners a high-five (two people face each other and touch palms and fingers high in the air). They should then tell their partners what they do for fun. These people will always be their high-five partners.

4. Then tell participants to quickly find their handshake partners and tell these partners about the high-five partners they just met (no music).
5. Now tell partners you will play the music again while they move around to find new partners. When the music stops, they will partner up, introduce themselves, and give these partners pats on the back. Partners should then share something they are proud of. These people will always be their pats-on-the-back partners.
6. Then tell participants to find their high-five partners and tell them about the pats-on-the-back partners they just met (no music).
7. Instruct participants that this time when they hear the music they should wave goodbye to their partners and return to their seats.

Processing the Activity

• Ask for volunteers to introduce their "pats-on-the-back" partners to the whole group.
• Ask for participants to share something interesting they learned about one of their partners.

Trainer/Facilitator Insights

_____

_____

_____

_____

_____

_____

_____

_____

Sharing Information

About Me

Common Denominator

Family Tree

Four Things I Want to Share

My Story

Patchwork Quilt

Pot of Gold

Self-Portrait

State Your Business

The Story of My Life

Who Am I?

➤ About Me

Purpose   This activity offers participants a way of getting acquainted that incorporates movement.

Risk Level   Low

Time   20 minutes

Number of Participants   Thirty maximum

Materials/Preparation
- Index cards, five per participant
- A pen or pencil for each participant
- Five sheets of flip chart paper; write one of the following categories at the top of each piece of flip chart paper, and post on walls of training room: SPORT, MODE OF TRAVEL, ARTICLE OF CLOTHING, FOOD, TYPE OF BUILDING
- Masking tape placed near the chart paper

Directions
1. Distribute five index cards and a pen or pencil to each participant.
2. Tell participants to visit each category posted around the room and decide what thing best describes them within that category.

   Note: Participants should take no more than 3 minutes to visit each category.

3. Instruct them to write their name and the thing that describes them on one of the index cards and the reason for their choice at the bottom of the card. Give an example: "I am a race car because I move fast."

4. Tell them to tape the card to the chart paper. They should place one index card on each category.
5. Ask for volunteers to share the reasons why they are like a particular sport, mode of travel, and so on.

Processing the Activity

- Point out that some people with the same choices had different explanations for them.
- Ask if it is easier or more difficult to share personal information this way and why this may be true.

Trainer/Facilitator Insights

_____

_____

_____

_____

_____

_____

_____

_____

➤ Common Denominator

Purpose   This activity directs participants to find something in common with others in their groups.

Risk Level   Low

Time   20 minutes

Number of Participants   Thirty-six maximum (in small groups of six)

Materials/Preparation
- Index cards with one of the following categories written on each card: Home, Family, Recreation, Education, Food, and Celebrations. Hobbies, Travel, and Pets can be used as additional categories. (Add more categories for larger numbers of participants.)

Directions
1. Break participants into small groups. Distribute index cards, one per small group.
2. Instruct participants to find two or more things in common with other group members pertaining to their category.
3. Ask groups to report to the larger group what the group members found they had in common.

Processing the Activity
- Ask participants how difficult or easy it was to find common denominators in their groups.
- Ask how finding commonalities among people helps in relating to one another.
- Ask how differences build a more diverse team.

Trainer/Facilitator Insights

_____

_____

_____

_____

_____

_____

_____

_____

➤ Family Tree

Purpose   This activity requires participants to introduce themselves by sharing their heritage.

Risk Level   Low to Moderate

Time   25 minutes

Number of Participants   Unlimited (in small groups of five to seven)

Materials/Preparation
- None

Directions
1. Ask participants to form small groups of five to seven members.
2. Tell participants that they will be introducing themselves to others in their small groups by sharing their heritages—their ancestors, homelands, languages, occupations, and historical tidbits about their families.
3. Give an example by sharing something of your own heritage.
4. Explain that each group member will have just 3 minutes to share.

Processing the Activity
- Ask why knowing someone's heritage can be helpful.
- Ask for volunteers to share something they learned about another group member.

Trainer/Facilitator Insights

_____

_____

_____

_____

_____

_____

_____

_____

➤ Four Things I Want to Share

Purpose   This activity offers a low-risk way for participants to share information about themselves.

Risk Level   Low

Time   20 minutes

Number of Participants   Unlimited

Materials/Preparation
- Plain paper (four pieces per participant)
- A marker or pen for each participant
- Masking tape available for participants

Directions
1. Give everyone four pieces of paper and a marker or pen. Instruct participants to write four different things they would like others to know about them, on each of the four separate pieces of paper (5 minutes).
2. Have them tape the papers to themselves, one each on their chest, shoulders, and back.
3. Tell participants to walk around the room mingling with other participants.
4. Instruct them to ask at least one question about each piece of paper they read (12 minutes).

Processing the Activity
- Ask for volunteers to share what they learned about others in the group.
- Ask whether there were commonalities in the things people shared about themselves.

Trainer/Facilitator Insights

_____

_____

_____

_____

_____

_____

_____

_____

➤ My Story

Purpose   This activity allows participants to create a story that helps describe who they are.

Risk Level   Low

Time   25 minutes

Number of Participants   Unlimited (in small groups of six to ten)

Materials/Preparation
- Copies of the My Story: Descriptive Word Sheet, with words cut into individual pieces
- Envelopes containing one set each of the cut-up words, one for each small group
- Large index cards (6 × 10), one per participant
- Tape and glue for each group

Directions
1. After participants are in groups, distribute envelopes containing the descriptive words, one to each small group. Also hand out index cards to each participant and tape and glue to each group.
2. Explain that the envelopes contain words that participants will use to describe themselves.
3. Tell them to write their names at the top of the cards and then choose words that can tell a story about who they are (10 minutes). Give an example: "I like eating soup and reading in winter. I often walk on the beach at dawn."
4. Tell them to stick the words to their index cards in story form.
5. When they have completed their cards, ask them to share their stories with their small groups (10 minutes).

Processing the Activity

- Ask the small groups whether anyone had a particularly creative story.
- Ask for volunteers to share something they learned about another person.
- Instruct participants to use tape to put their index cards in place of their name tags or ask them to post the cards on the walls of the training room to be read later.
- If time permits, ask participants to circulate and share their stories with people in other groups.

Trainer/Facilitator Insights

_____

_____

_____

_____

_____

_____

_____

_____

My Story: Descriptive Words Sheet

Indoors	Ball games	Water	Play	Ability	Reaching
Outside	Dancing	Colorful	Thrifty	Bright	Achievement
Reading	Smart	Proud	Worker	Lively	Fly
Run	Movies	Devout	Advocating	Soup	Chocolate
Sky	Losing	Greatest	Plane	Hoping	Eating
Curious	Restaurants	Shop	Peace	Dazzle	Careful
Happy	Free Spirit	Survivor	Sharing	Picture	Like
Jokester	Intense	Emotional	Ice cream	Coffee	Race
Serious	Playful	Excitable	Inventive	Favorite	Try
Studious	Cooking	Fun	Leap	Promise	Home
Athlete	Artist	Glad	Singing	Car	Sense
Handy	Gardener	Creative	Driving	Taste	Honest
Clever	Simplicity	Passionate	Cat	Feel	Experience
Mother	Sibling	Children	Writing	Pizza	Dramatic
Father	Journal	Games	Leading	Drink	Computer
Friend	Hearing	Gorgeous	Pleasure	Life	Companion
Bike	Wine	Wise	Sunshine	Studying	Teach
Poetry	Boat	Witty	Moonlight	Softness	Iced tea
Snow	Dog	Rowdy	Spouse	Flowers	French fries
Warm	Walking	Talk	Sleeping	Live	Fan
TV	Beach	Listen	Caressing	Books	Learn
Music	Mountains	Fit	Conscientious	Light	Sun
Stars	Darkness	Dawn	Dusk	Peanuts	Butter

➤ Patchwork Quilt

Purpose   This activity gives participants the opportunity to share
their differences.

Risk Level   Low to Moderate

Time   35 minutes

Number of Participants   Unlimited (in small groups of six to eight)

Materials/Preparation
- Felt-tipped markers, one set per group
- Scissors
- Glue sticks
- A good supply of colored paper, 8 ½ × 11, per group
- Flip chart paper, one sheet per group
- Masking tape

Directions
1. Tell participants that each group will make a diversity quilt with
   the supplies provided.
2. Explain that each group member should make one piece for the
   quilt that describes or symbolizes his/her uniqueness
   (10 minutes).
3. Once group members have completed their pieces of the quilt,
   ask them to share their quilt pieces within their groups
   (10 minutes).
4. Tell groups to make the quilt using the chart paper for backing
   and stick their pieces in crazy-quilt design on the paper. They
   should then use masking tape to "hang" the quilts around the
   room (5 minutes).
5. Instruct participants to take a few minutes to walk around the
   room viewing each group's quilts (5 minutes).

Processing the Activity

- Ask for volunteers to share their observations about the quilts they viewed.
- Tell participants that they can take advantage of breaks to seek people out who have quilt pieces that interest them.

Trainer/Facilitator Insights

_____

_____

_____

_____

_____

_____

_____

_____

➤ Pot of Gold

Purpose   This activity allows participants to consider what they
   bring to the group or training that will help with today's topic.

Risk Level   Moderate

Time   20 minutes

Number of Participants   Thirty

Materials/Preparation
   • Small pieces of yellow paper, one per participant
   • A pen or pencil for each participant
   • A large pot or bowl

Directions
   1. Tell participants that each of them brings experiences and talents
      to the group or training. Give examples that relate to the work of
      the group as follows: "Our topic is conflict resolution, and some-
      one here may have served as a mediator or been involved in the
      conflict resolution process. Another may have the ability to
      summarize group discussion. Still another may be a good
      listener."
   2. Distribute the paper and pens or pencils to participants.
   3. Instruct each participant to write something he or she brings to
      the session on a piece of the yellow paper and bring it to the pot
      at the front of the room.
   4. After everyone has contributed, move around the room and ask
      each participant, in turn, to draw a piece of paper from the pot
      and read it aloud.

Processing the Activity

- Ask whether anyone was surprised at the diversity of responses and why.
- Ask in what ways people with diverse talents and interests can make a strong team.

Trainer/Facilitator Insights

_____

_____

_____

_____

_____

_____

_____

_____

◢ Self-Portrait

Purpose   This activity allows participants to share some things about themselves and receive positive feedback from others.

Risk Level   Low to Moderate

Time   20 minutes

Number of Participants   Unlimited (in small groups of six to eight)

Materials/Preparation
- Legal-size plain white paper
- Markers and crayons
- Masking tape

Directions
1. Distribute a piece of paper to each participant. Give each small group drawing materials.
2. Instruct participants to make self-portraits and include three things about themselves in the portrait. Tell them they can use stick figures if they wish. Their names should be on the portraits (10 minutes).
3. Ask participants to share their portraits within their small groups.
4. Once groups have completed sharing, have all participants post their portraits on the walls of the training room with masking tape.
5. Tell participants that they will be getting to know each other better as the training progresses.
6. Explain that at various times during the training session, participants can write their observations about other group members on the portraits belonging to those people. Observations should be positive. Give an example: "If you

notice that one group member is especially friendly, you can write the word 'friendly' on his or her portrait."

7. Remind participants prior to breaks about adding their observations to the portraits.

Processing the Activity

- See the Self-Portrait Continued activity in the Adjourning section.

Trainer/Facilitator Insights

_____

_____

_____

_____

_____

_____

_____

_____

➤ State Your Business

Purpose   This activity allows participants to share some of their personal history with others.

Risk Level   Low

Time   25 minutes

Number of Participants   Unlimited

Materials/Preparation
- Legal-size paper, one piece per participant
- Markers, one per participant
- Masking tape

Directions
1. Distribute paper and markers.
2. Ask participants to draw an outline of the state in which they were born. Ask them to draw a star in the place within the state where they were born.
3. Tell them to list three things related to their place of birth that are part of their personal history (10 minutes). Give an example: "I was born in Boston, Massachusetts, and grew up just outside of Boston. One of my ancestors rode with Paul Revere. The train was my favorite mode of transportation when I was growing up."
4. Instruct participants to use masking tape to post their papers on the wall and then to walk around reading others' information (5 minutes).

Processing the Activity
- Ask participants what they found in common with other people.
- Tell participants to seek out people during breaks in the training who are from places they might like to visit or learn more about.

Trainer/Facilitator Insights

_____

_____

_____

_____

_____

_____

_____

_____

⊇ The Story of My Life

Purpose   This activity allows participants to share by creating a book jacket.

Risk Level   Low to Moderate

Time   30 minutes

Number of Participants   Forty maximum (in small groups of five or six)

Materials/Preparation
- Heavy sheets of paper, one per participant (11 × 17, if possible)
- Markers in a variety of colors for each small group

Directions
1. Distribute the sheets of paper and markers within the small groups.
2. Ask participants how they would title books about their lives thus far.
3. Instruct them to design a book jacket that includes that title (15 minutes).
4. Once the book jackets are complete, ask participants to share the reasons for what they put on their book jackets within their small groups.

Processing the Activity
- Ask participants in each group to share a particularly interesting "life story" they heard.
- Ask if it was difficult to write a few words to summarize a whole life, and why.

Trainer/Facilitator Insights

_____

_____

_____

_____

_____

_____

_____

_____

➤ Who Am I?

Purpose   This activity is designed to help participants to become better acquainted.

Risk Level   Low

Time   15 minutes

Number of Participants   Unlimited

Materials/Preparation   None

Directions
1. Instruct participants to find partners.
2. Explain that they will be identifying three items currently in their possession that are symbols of who they are.
3. Tell them they can use items they are wearing, such as jewelry, and items they have in their purses or wallets; for example, a participant might choose a pencil, a watch, and a phone card. The pencil symbolizes the participant's efforts to write a book, the watch symbolizes the participant's tendency to be late for appointments, and the phone card represents family who live in another state.
4. Instruct participants to place the three items they choose on the table in front of them.
5. Partners will take turns guessing what the items tell about the person.
6. Tell participants they will have 2 minutes to guess what their partners' items symbolize. At the end of 2 minutes their partners should explain what the items actually symbolize.
7. Tell the pairs that one partner should begin guessing what his or her partner's items symbolize.

8. Notify participants when 2 minutes are up, and give the first partner a few seconds to explain what his or her items symbolize.
9. Next, tell the first partners that they now have 2 minutes to guess what their partner's items symbolize.
10. Notify participants when 2 minutes are up, and tell the second partner to explain what his or her items symbolize.

Processing the Activity
- Ask for volunteers to share their experience with the activity.
- Ask participants what they learned about their partners that surprised them.

Trainer/Facilitator Insights

_____

_____

_____

_____

_____

_____

_____

➤ Section 2
Storming

Why is the storming stage of group development important? Because without it participants will never get past the issues and agendas they brought with them and be able to move to the real work of the team. As stated in the last section, people arrive at training sessions, groups, and teams as individuals, with unique needs and expectations. This stage brings individuals to the point at which they must come to terms with the differences between their expectations and those of others and the fact that their needs may not be met in the way they expected. The storming stage is brought on by differences in communication styles, diversity of group members, clashing personal agendas, and differing perspectives, all typical of newly formed groups. People who are together only once, for a short training or meeting, will not move to the storming stage. Groups that reach this stage have had ongoing interaction, whether in a week-long training or in regular group meetings.

Conflict at this stage is normal. The management of conflict defines how the rest of the group's work will proceed. The activities in this section address these issues by allowing participants to explore their own and others' ideas in structured ways.

Participant Behaviors

The approaches of some participants to this stage are low-key. For example, some groups have members who express their concerns in non-threatening ways, allowing for a discussion and the resolution of a particular issue. This nonthreatening approach most often motivates others to speak up, bringing more issues to light, with the same positive result. Ultimately, participants who experience this kind of storming will recognize that the honesty and openness expressed in the group has moved them forward in their ability to relate effectively with one another.

Other groups or teams may have more volatile participants, who make judgmental statements that put others on the defensive. When this happens, participants begin to take comments from others as personal affronts and may respond accordingly. You can probably tell what kind of group you have before they reach this stage. Give more volatile groups opportunities to experience the diversity, the different perspectives, and communications problems in structured and non-threatening ways using the activities in this book. This approach will do a great deal to defuse potential confrontations.

As they are working through this stage, remind participants that it is natural to disagree and that focusing on the resolution of the discord will help them move forward with their work.

Other Uses for Storming Activities

The activities in this section are useful for promoting communication skills, practicing conflict resolution, and exploring diversity and one's own ideas and feelings as well as those of others. It is not necessary for a group to be at the Storming stage of development to be involved in many of the activities included here. For example, the "Personal Space" activity explores relationships and would be useful in work with families. The "What It's Like . . ." activity could be used to train health aides or educators.

In addition, communication activities found in this section are useful for groups and teams at every stage of development as well as for short training of groups from a single workplace. A school, for example, may want to include a communication activity in a curriculum training for teachers. A staff meeting at a small company could include a communication activity as a way of getting the meeting started.

Common Issues in Training and Group Work

What if . . .

- *Very reserved participants begin to show discomfort with the conflict?* Remind everyone that the storming stage is a normal part of group development. Encourage participants to be considerate of those people in their group who find conflict threatening. Ask the individual what the group can do to help him or her feel more at ease. Leaders and trainers can also approach uncomfortable participants individually, to provide reassurance or give them the option to remove themselves from the group during this time.

- *The whole group is expressing discontent?* Start the group brainstorming lists of the things that concern them or are frustrating them. Written concerns lack the drama that is present in a voiced concern. Review the list, encouraging ideas and solutions from the group. This response should mellow the group and direct them toward problem solving. If possible, work until participants can bring closure to their key concerns. Otherwise, use the "parking lot" approach, writing concerns on posted chart paper and addressing them before the conclusion of the training or meeting. *An example of this kind of storming is participants disagreeing about everything, from the quality of the snacks to the important issues.*

- *There is a definite difference of opinion between races, genders, or work positions?* Point it out. Note that differing perspectives come from different experiences. Say that it is not necessary to agree, only to recognize and accept differences. *One example would be support staff people declaring that management's expectations of them far exceed the support staff's job descriptions. The management, in this case, strongly disagrees.*

- *A participant becomes very outspoken?* Thank the person for sharing his thoughts and say that you and he can deal with the issue at the break/end of the training. If he still does not back down and is causing a disturbance, give the class a break. You may end up giving the participant an opportunity to withdraw from the training. *An example of this kind of participant is the person who continues to raise his or her voice over the voice of the trainer or facilitator, or stands at an inappropriate time, which can be a sign of aggression.*

- *You have one person who is very strong in trying to direct the training toward his or her personal agenda?* Thank the person for sharing and say that the issue is for another training on another day. If the individual persists, continue to remind him or her that you need to stay on subject. You may have to speak to this individual alone. If you do, ask the participant to check to see whether the training material is appropriate to his or her interests. *One example is the feminist who is trying to insert gender discrimination into a time-management training.*

- *A participant talks too much?* Gently interrupt. Say that you need to hear from others. Hold your hand up toward the participant while seeking responses from others. Take the person aside and ask that he or she speak less and listen more. *Note:* These people are often motivated by a need for attention. Giving them recognition in almost any form can help calm them down.

- *People persist in having side conversations?* As you are speaking to the group, move and stand behind those individuals while continuing to talk. They will quickly realize that all eyes in the room are on them. You can also just stop speaking. Let the silence point up their noisy whispering.

- *People are sleeping, working on other things, or otherwise obviously uninvolved in the training?* Ask the sleepers if they are ill or invite the room to stand and stretch. You can also tell the whole group that some folks are on task, but the task is from a different training. Explain that those that are busy doing other work during the training will not receive certification, credit, or other recognition at the end of the training. Another way to ensure participants are with you is to walk around the room regularly, standing over groups and individuals as they do their work. *Note:* Remember that you are working with adults. Publicly correcting adults embarrasses them and creates hostile participants.

Communication and Conflict

Across a Crowded Room

Can You Remember?

Can You Remember? II

Give a Sign

Giving Directions

How Are You Doing?

OK or Not OK?

Picture Search

Practice, Practice

Without Context

➤ Across a Crowded Room

Purpose   This activity explores how personal space affects communication.

Risk Level   Moderate

Time   15 minutes

Number of Participants   Forty maximum

Materials/Preparation   None

Space Requirements   Open space free of tables and chairs

Directions
1. Instruct participants to find partners.
2. Tell partners to move to opposite sides of the room.
3. Ask participants what kind of communication can appropriately take place from this distance.
4. Ask them to demonstrate the kind of communication they think works with this distance. (Most participants will wave or call out "hello.")
5. Instruct participants to move closer together for a friendly casual conversation. Partners should decide how far apart they should be.
6. Ask participants to converse at that distance.
7. Next, ask partners to demonstrate the distance needed between them for personal sharing.
8. Finally, ask them to position themselves with their partners for a heated discussion.

Processing the Activity

- Tell participants that individuals define personal space differently. Ask if there were distances between themselves and their partners that made them uncomfortable.
- Ask them whether they have those uncomfortable experiences in the workplace.
- Ask whether there are differences between the work environment and being with friends and family in terms of their personal space.

Trainer/Facilitator Insights

_____

_____

_____

_____

_____

_____

_____

➤ Can You Remember?

Purpose   This activity helps participants experience the limitations of exclusively auditory communication.

Risk Level   Low

Time   20 minutes

Number of Participants   Twenty maximum

Materials/Preparation   None

Space Requirements   An open area free of tables and chairs

Directions

1. Instruct participants to find partners.
2. Tell the partners to turn so that one partner is facing the other's back.
3. Explain that for 3 minutes, the partner in the back will tell the other partner about a personal experience that was especially meaningful or exciting.
4. Say that, while the one partner is speaking, the other will walk away. The speaking partner will follow, continuing to share the special experience.
5. At the end of 3 minutes, the listening partner should share as much as he or she remembers about the other partner's story with that partner.
6. Ask partners to change roles, and proceed as before.
7. At the end of 3 minutes, again ask the listening partner to talk about what he or she heard with his or her partner.
8. Ask for volunteers to share their experiences with talking and with listening during this activity with the entire group.

Processing the Activity

- Ask participants why this activity is easier for some people than for others. (Auditory learners have an easier time with this activity than visual learners.)
- Ask what cues to communication were absent during this activity (eye contact, facial expressions, lips moving).
- Ask how it feels to have someone walk away when you are speaking to them.

Trainer/Facilitator Insights

_____

_____

_____

_____

_____

_____

_____

_____

➤ Can You Remember? II

Purpose   This activity helps participants experience the limits of visual communication.

Risk Level   Low

Time   20 minutes

Number of Participants   Forty maximum

Materials/Preparation
- An uncommon or unfamiliar piece of artwork that is not abstract
- Paper and a pencil for each participant

Directions
1. Tell participants that you will slowly walk around the room, giving each person a chance to view a piece of artwork.
2. Show the artwork to everyone in the room without speaking.
3. Put the artwork away, hand out paper and pencils, and ask participants to make a list of the things they remember about the work.
4. Ask for volunteers to share their lists.
5. Display the artwork again so that participants can see how well they remembered it.

Processing the Activity
- Ask participants why some people did better than others. (Visual learners usually do better than auditory learners.)
- Ask what clues were missing in this exclusively visual exercise (words, reactions, comments, voice tones, and hand motions).

Trainer/Facilitator Insights

_____

_____

_____

_____

_____

_____

_____

_____

➤ Give a Sign

Purpose This activity gives participants the opportunity to practice communicating in their workplaces.

Risk Level Moderate

Time 30 minutes

Number of Participants Unlimited (in small groups of six to eight)

Materials/Preparation
- White or colored poster paper cut in pieces (9×9 is a good size), one per participant
- Colored markers

Directions
1. Distribute the index paper, one piece per participant, and markers.
2. Tell participants that they will be designing a sign that will communicate something to others in their workplaces.
3. Explain that this communication should relate to something they would like to say to co-workers. Explain, "For example, if you get a large number of interruptions during your day, you may want to make a sign that reads 'Do Not Disturb So Often.'"
4. Once participants have completed their signs, ask them to share in small groups.
5. Ask for volunteers to share signs from their groups that they considered especially clever or relevant.

Processing the Activity
- Ask if anyone used his or her sign to communicate something that is difficult to say. If so, ask how it felt to put it in writing.
- Ask participants what other way they can impart the information if putting up a sign is not an option.

Trainer/Facilitator Insights

_____

_____

_____

_____

_____

_____

_____

_____

➤ Giving Directions

Purpose   This activity allows participants to practice communicating precise information.

Risk Level   Low to Moderate

Time   35 minutes

Number of Participants   Twenty maximum

Materials/Preparation
- Plain paper, $8^1/_2 \times 11$
- A pen or pencil for each participant

Space Requirements   Training room in a building that allows participants to move in the halls and around the grounds

Directions
1. Tell participants that they will be taking a 20-minute break that will include preparation for an activity.
2. Prior to the break, instruct participants to identify a secret spot in the hall or on the grounds and prepare to write directions to this spot.
3. After the break, hand out paper and pencils and instruct participants to write the directions to their secret spots. They should not name their spots.
4. Collect the directions participants have written, shuffle them, and redistribute.
5. Tell participants that they have 5 minutes to find the secret spot from the directions. After 5 minutes, they should return to the training room.

Processing the Activity
- Ask for volunteers who had no trouble finding the secret spots to describe the directions they received.

- Ask how many people have encountered directions or
  information that was difficult to understand. Ask why it was
  difficult.

Trainer/Facilitator Insights

_____

_____

_____

_____

_____

_____

_____

_____

➤ How Are You Doing?

Purpose   This activity allows participants to explore different forms of communicating.

Risk Level   Low

Time   20 minutes

Number of Participants   Unlimited (small groups of six to eight)

Materials/Preparation
- Flip chart paper and a marker
- Masking tape
- A flip chart page with the following list written on it: sympathy, birthday, happy event (birth or wedding), illness, holiday, divorce, promotion
- Markers for each small group

Directions
1. With the whole group, brainstorm a list of ways people communicate and list the ideas on chart paper. (Ideas should include visit, phone, fax, e-mail, and letters.)
2. Use masking tape to post the event list and the brainstorm list so that they are visible to all groups.
3. Tell participants to discuss in their groups the best way of communicating the feelings or thoughts related to any of the events on the list. Someone in the group should record their choices.
4. Ask one group to share their list with the larger group. Each time they read a choice, ask how many other groups agreed with them.
5. Ask groups that did not agree what they thought was a better choice.
6. Continue down the events list in this manner.

Processing the Activity
- Discuss the pros and cons of different forms of communicating.
- Ask whether there are differences in the way participants communicate in and out of the workplace. What are they?

Trainer/Facilitator Insights

_____

_____

_____

_____

_____

_____

_____

_____

➤ OK or Not OK?

Purpose   This activity gives participants the opportunity to explore questionable behaviors that occur in the workplace.

Risk Level   Moderate to High

Time   20 minutes

Number of Participants   Unlimited (small groups of six to eight)

Materials/Preparation
- Small strips of paper stating the different behaviors listed here, one per group:
  - Hugging
  - Ethnic or religious jokes or comments
  - Off-color jokes
  - Patting (any part of a person's body)
  - Neck/Shoulder massage
  - Personal body references
  - Sexist comments
    (Add others that may be an issue for the group)
- Flip chart paper
- Markers
- Masking tape

Directions
1. Distribute a behavior statement to each small group along with a piece of flip chart paper and markers.
2. Explain that there are behaviors that occur in every workplace that people may find offensive or uncomfortable.
3. Ask groups to discuss their behavior statement. They should talk about when the behavior is "OK" and "not OK" and how to address the "not OK" behavior. Allow 10 minutes for this part of the activity.
4. Instruct groups to list their thoughts and their solutions on flip chart paper and post them on a wall of the training room using masking tape.
5. Tell groups to move around the room, reading each group's posting.

Processing the Activity

- Ask participants if they noticed similarities among the reactions of the groups to the different behaviors.
- Ask them how better communication skills would solve some of these issues.
- Ask how they would respond differently if the behavior came from a supervisor/boss.

Trainer/Facilitator Insights

_____

_____

_____

_____

_____

_____

_____

_____

➤ Picture Search

Purpose   This activity encourages participants to practice effective communication with a partner.

Risk Level   Low

Time   25 minutes

Number of Participants   Unlimited (partnered)

Materials/Preparation
- Plain paper
- Colored markers
- A large table in the front of the room
- Small prizes (optional)

Directions
1. Instruct partners to separate and move to different parts of the room.
2. Tell each participant to make a picture of a house. Encourage them to use lots of color and detail. They should not put their names on their pictures.
3. Once they have completed their pictures, tell participants to bring them to the table at the front of the room. The pictures should be spread out as much as possible.
4. Tell participants to return to sit next to their partners.
5. Explain that one partner will describe his drawing to the other partner, who will then try to find it on the table. That participant will keep bringing back pictures to show his or her partner until he/she finds the right one.
6. Tell participants to repeat the process with the other partner.
7. Tell partners to raise their hands when they have found both pictures.
8. Give a small prize to the partners who found each other's pictures first (optional).

Processing the Activity

- Ask participants how communication affected their success in finding their partner's picture.
- Ask in what other situations communicating details might be important.

Trainer/Facilitator Insights

_____

_____

_____

_____

_____

_____

_____

_____

➤ Practice, Practice

Purpose   This activity allows participants to practice addressing conflicts.

Risk Level   Moderate to High

Time   40 minutes

Number of Participants   Thirty

Materials/Preparation
- A paper plate for each participant
- A pen or marker for each participant
- Masking tape

Directions
1. Instruct participants to find partners. Give each pair markers and paper plates.
2. Tell them to think of a difficulty they have either personally or professionally with another individual.
3. Instruct each partner to draw a face on his or her paper plate to represent that individual.
4. Have them move to a part of the room where they can tape their plates to the wall.
5. Explain that one partner should practice addressing the plate assertively as if it were the person with whom he or she is having difficulty. The other partner should observe and then give feedback. They should then switch. This should take about 5 minutes for each participant.
6. Suggest that participants practice again, using the feedback their partners provided.

Processing the Activity

- Ask participants why it is a good idea to practice what they will say to someone with whom they have a conflict. (Practicing helps reduce the likelihood that participants will speak impulsively and say hurtful or inappropriate things.)
- Ask participants why feedback from their partners can be helpful. (Feedback allows speakers to reflect on what they said and how they said it.)

Trainer/Facilitator Insights

_____

_____

_____

_____

_____

_____

_____

➤ Without Context

Purpose   This activity challenges participants to put something they hear into visual form.

Risk Level   Low to Moderate

Time   20 minutes

Number of Participants   Unlimited

Materials/Preparation
- Paper
- Colored markers, enough to allow each participant a variety of colors from which to choose
- A copy of Without Context: Story for the facilitator

Directions
1. Tell participants that one of the most difficult forms of communication is transferring information they hear into visual form.
2. Hand out paper and markers. Explain that you will be reading a brief story. Once participants have heard the story, they should draw what they remember about it in detail. For example, if the story has a green ball in it, they should draw the ball and color it green.
3. Read the story, then have participants draw.
4. Once they have completed their pictures, explain that you will read the story again and they can check what they have accurately included in their pictures.
5. Ask for volunteers to share how well they remembered the story.

Processing the Activity

- Ask participants why many of them had trouble remembering the story accurately. (Visual learners have the greatest difficulty with this activity. In addition, people remember best when they hear something that is in context with what they already know or that they can connect to other things. Often people need to hear things in many different ways for it to sink in.)
- Ask participants what this understanding of listening and learning means to them in their workplace or personal life. One example might be that telling a child something once would not be effective. Or telling that child something without relating it to his or her life would not be effective.

Trainer/Facilitator Insights

_____

_____

_____

_____

_____

_____

_____

_____

Without Context: Story

An old brown shack sat at the edge of a pine forest. It had a gray tin roof slightly mottled with rust. Smoke rose from the chimney and curled back into the trees. Tiny yellow crocuses bloomed in a small garden next to a freshly painted red door. A round green table and two old black chairs were set under a blooming cherry tree as if waiting for diners. A clothesline was attached to one side of the shack; a blue shirt hung there flapped in the breeze. On the other side of the shack was a rosebush, full of bright red buds.

Diversity

Birth Order

Discrimination

Gender Specific

In Someone Else's Shoes

We're All Human

What It's Like . . .

➤ Birth Order

Purpose   This activity gives participants the opportunity to look at their birth orders in terms of personality development and how it helps or hinders them in the workplace.

Risk Level   Moderate

Time   30 minutes

Number of Participants   Forty maximum

Materials/Preparation
- Four large cards or pieces of poster paper with the following written on them: OLDEST, YOUNGEST, MIDDLE, ONLY

Directions
1. Post the cards in different areas of the room.
2. Instruct participants to stand under the card appropriate to their birth order or the closest to it. For example, the fourth child of six children would stand under the MIDDLE card.
3. Ask them to discuss within their groups traits they think may be characteristic of oldest, youngest, middle, or only children.
4. Ask each group what personality traits they found in common.
5. Instruct them to discuss how these traits help or hinder them in the workplace.

Processing the Activity
- Ask what would happen if the workplace was made up completely of only children.
- Ask how diverse personalities benefit the workplace.

Trainer/Facilitator Insights

_____

_____

_____

_____

_____

_____

_____

_____

➤ Discrimination

Purpose   This activity allows participants to share experiences they have had with prejudice and discrimination.

Risk Level   High

Time   30 minutes

Number of Participants   Unlimited (small groups of eight to ten)

Materials/Preparation
- A board or flip chart with the following written on it: Race, Gender, Religion, Politics, Physical Disability, Language/Nationality, Economic Status, Age

Directions
1. Place participants in small groups. Explain to them that many people experience being discriminated against every day.
2. Tell participants to select a topic from the board and share with their small groups an experience they had and their feelings associated with it. If participants cannot recall an experience with discrimination, suggest they share one they witnessed and the feelings of being a witness.
3. Ask for volunteers from the groups to share their experiences and the associated feelings with the larger group.

Processing the Activity
- Ask participants whether anyone learned something new from this activity.
- Ask them how awareness can help avoid discrimination.
- Ask participants how discrimination in the workplace affects the work environment.

Trainer/Facilitator Insights

➤ Gender Specific

Purpose   This activity helps participants to explore gender stereotyping.

Risk Level   Moderate to High

Time   20 minutes

Number of Participants   Thirty maximum (balance number of males and females)

Materials/Preparation
- Toys most often considered female, as follows: dolls, tea sets, plastic cookware, dress-up clothes, jewelry, make-up, and so on
- Toys most often considered male, as follows: trucks, cars, planes, balls, plastic tools, toy weapons, action figures, and so forth

Directions
1. Divide participants into two groups by gender.
2. Distribute the toys most often considered female to the male group. Distribute the toys most often considered male to the female group.
3. Ask the groups to play with the toys for 3 minutes.
4. Instruct them to create a story around some of the toys from the perspective of the opposite gender. For example, the male group might make up a story about the little girl who invited all her dolls to tea.
5. Invite each group to share the story they created.
6. Applaud all efforts.

Processing the Activity
- Ask for volunteers to share how comfortable or uncomfortable they were when doing this activity and why that was.
- Ask participants what effect gender stereotyping can have on a workplace.

Trainer/Facilitator Insights

_____

_____

_____

_____

_____

_____

_____

_____

➤ In Someone Else's Shoes

Purpose   This activity is intended to help participants explore different perspectives.

Risk Level   Low to Moderate

Time   30 minutes

Number of Participants   Unlimited (small groups of six to eight)

Materials/Preparation
- Copy of the In Someone Else's Shoes: Historical Figures and Current Issues sheet on a piece of chart paper posted where all groups can see it
- Paper and a pencil for each group

Directions
1. Explain that it can help us in our work relationships to practice looking at the world from another person's perspective.
2. Ask each group to choose a historical figure from the posted list and an issue that they would like their figure to comment on from his or her own perspective. *Note:* Groups may choose figures or issues not listed.
3. Tell the groups to first discuss their person—when he or she lived and what kind of world existed at that time. They can imagine what they do not know for sure.
4. Once they have a clear idea of who their person was, tell the groups to write short commentaries, imagining that their historical figure is expressing his or her own viewpoint about the issue the group chose.
5. Invite each group to present its commentary.

Processing the Activity
- Ask groups to share any struggles they had putting themselves in their historical figure's shoes.
- Ask for volunteers to share how being able to look at an issue from different perspectives affects a person's life.

Trainer/Facilitator Insights

_____

_____

_____

_____

_____

_____

_____

_____

In Someone Else's Shoes: Historical Figures and Current Issues

Historical Figures

Gandhi

Mozart

Davy Crockett

Florence Nightingale

Thomas Edison

Benjamin Franklin

Amelia Earhart

Rudolph Valentino

Emily Dickinson

Lewis and Clark

George Washington Carver

Current Issues

Terrorism

Today's Music

Environment vs. Development

Cloning

Technology and Personal Privacy

Energy Resources

Space Travel, Present and Future

Current Film Ratings

Television's Use in the Home

Alaskan Oil

Agriculture

➤ We're All Human

Purpose   This activity gives participants the opportunity to explore the differences and similarities among human beings.

Risk Level   Low to Moderate

Time   20 minutes

Number of Participants   Thirty (small groups of five to six)

Materials/Preparation
- Flip chart paper, one piece per small group
- Markers for each small group
- Masking tape

Directions
1. Distribute a piece of blank flip chart paper and markers to each small group.
2. Instruct participants to draw some semblance of a human figure on their paper.
3. Tell them to brainstorm what they believe are the needs, wants, and feelings of all human beings and record their ideas around the figure they have drawn.
4. Ask each small group to share their work with the larger group.

Processing the Activity
- Ask what the findings of the group say about us as human beings. (We are more alike than different, have similar basic needs, wants, and feelings.)
- Ask how participants can use this information in the workplace.

Trainer/Facilitator Insights

_____

_____

_____

_____

_____

_____

_____

_____

➤ What It's Like . . .

Purpose   This activity is intended to provide the participants with the experience of someone with an impairment or handicap.

Risk Level   Moderate to High

Time   20 to 30 minutes

Number of Participants   Unlimited

Materials/Preparation
- Plain paper, three pieces per participant
- A pencil for each participant

Directions
1. Distribute paper and pencils to participants.
2. Tell participants that you will be providing some instructions and that they must follow all instructions and cannot ask questions.
3. Say to participants, "List four makinpoppers on a piece of paper. Beside each makinpopper, you should write everything you can about foofoo and gooble. When you have finished, ginch ter massin."
4. When they have finished writing, ask participants what it was like to listen to instructions they didn't understand.
5. Next, instruct participants to punch two small holes in a piece of paper. The holes should be parallel and about the same distance apart as their eyes.
6. Instruct participants to hold the paper to their eyes while reading a section of the training material. Designate the portion of material they should read.
7. Interrupt the reading process to ask participants how it is going. Ask them what feelings they are experiencing trying to read the material.

8. Next, instruct participants to write down the information you will be giving them using their nondominant hand.
9. Choose information that is important to the training and read it aloud. Read at a normal pace and do not repeat. For example, after the training, they may need to send their certificates of completion to a particular address to get credit for the training.

Processing the Activity

- Ask for volunteers to share the feelings they experienced during this activity.
- Ask for volunteers to share any new learning that occurred as a result of the activity and how it might affect a workplace.

Trainer/Facilitator Insights

_____

_____

_____

_____

_____

_____

_____

_____

Exploring Ideas and Feelings

All About Groups

As Others See Me

Comfort Level

Feelings Behind the Words

Personal Space

Risky Business

Stress, Stress, Stress

What Do You See?

Whoops!

➤ All About Groups

Purpose This activity encourages participants to explore group dynamics.

Risk Level Moderate

Time 30 minutes

Number of Participants Unlimited

Materials/Preparation None

Space Requirements Enough space for participants to move around freely

Directions
1. Explain to participants that they will be forming groups according to a variety of criteria.
2. Tell participants to form [number] groups according to similar physical characteristics other than gender or ethnicity.

   Note: The number of groups you ask them to form will depend on the size of the group. For example, if there are thirty participants, you can ask them to form five groups of six participants each.

3. Ask participants what kind of dynamics may occur in the workplace when people form these kinds of groups. (Grouping people with the same physical characteristics makes it easy to leave people out.)
4. Next tell participants to form [number] groups that have similar skills. This grouping process will take some time and discussion.
5. Ask participants what may happen in the workplace when people form these kinds of groups. (A hierarchy may develop in a workplace.)

6. Instruct participants to form [number] groups that create their own reasons for existing.
7. Ask participants what may happen in the workplace when people form these groups. (Separation and exclusivity may occur in the workplace.)

Processing the Activity

- Ask participants what kinds of groups they experience in their workplace.

Trainer/Facilitator Insights

_____

_____

_____

_____

_____

_____

_____

_____

➤ As Others See Me

Purpose   This activity allows participants the opportunity to learn how others see them. The activity is designed for participants who already know one another.

Risk Level   High

Time   25 minutes

Number of Participants   Unlimited (partnered)

Materials/Preparation
- Plain paper, $8\frac{1}{2} \times 11$, one piece for each participant
- Markers

Directions
1. Give participants paper and markers and ask them to form into pairs.
2. Tell participants that they are to draw caricatures of their partners, stressing their positive characteristics. Emphasize that they do not have to be artistic to do this activity; they can use stick figures if necessary.
3. Instruct participants to share the drawings with their partners and explain what they drew. For example: "I gave you really big ears because you are such a good listener."

Processing the Activity
- Ask participants if anything they heard from their partners was a surprise.
- Ask them how it feels to be perceived by someone else in a way they may not have been expecting.

Trainer/Facilitator Insights

_____

_____

_____

_____

_____

_____

_____

_____

➤ Comfort Level

Purpose   This activity gives participants the opportunity to look at how they maintain a level of comfort in a new situation.

Risk Level   Moderate

Time   20 minutes

Number of Participants   Unlimited (small groups of six to eight)

Materials/Preparation   None

Directions
1. Ask participants to form small groups.
2. Tell them to recall where they sat when they arrived at the training session and to think about why they chose to sit where they did.
3. Ask them to share their reasons for choosing a particular seat within their small groups.
4. Ask for volunteers to share their reasons for choosing their seats with the larger group.

Processing the Activity
- Ask participants why human beings, as a general rule, choose comfort over risk or challenge.
- Ask participants how they feel when they take the risk of choosing a less comfortable situation.
- Ask them what may happen as a result of making a less comfortable choice. (Personal growth may occur.)

Trainer/Facilitator Insights

_____

_____

_____

_____

_____

_____

_____

_____

➤ Feelings Behind the Words

Purpose   This activity gives participants the opportunity to practice identifying feelings.

Risk Level   High

Time   25 minutes

Number of Participants   Unlimited (small groups of eight to ten)

Materials/Preparation
- A copy of the Feelings Behind the Words: Feelings statements sheet for each participant
- A pen or pencil for each participant

Directions
1. After forming participants into small groups, hand out the Feeling Statements sheets and pens or pencils.
2. Ask participants to work alone to identify the feelings they think may be behind each statement.
3. Once they have completed their Feelings Statements sheets, they should discuss each statement and the associated feelings within their small groups.

Processing the Activity
- Ask groups whether they disagreed about the feelings behind any of the statements and why.
- Ask what additional clues one might get about feelings from a spoken statement (facial expression, voice tone, and so on).
- Point out that feelings are neither right nor wrong and that recognizing the feelings behind the words may help us to suspend judgment about a speaker.

Trainer/Facilitator Insights

_____

_____

_____

_____

_____

_____

_____

_____

Feelings Behind the Words: Feelings Statements

I wish I could stay home from work tomorrow.

I really don't want to make a speech at the luncheon.

My boss is sending me to Vegas to present at the conference.

I quit smoking last year.

My sister is getting her test results back from the doctor today.

I have never told anyone before that I wear a back brace.

I didn't get the job.

The company wants me to manage their office in New York. It is a big promotion and a cross-country move.

➤ Personal Space

Purpose   This activity gives participants the opportunity to examine
relationships they have in the workplace and in their personal
lives.

Risk Level   Moderate

Time   20 minutes

Number of Participants   Unlimited (small groups of six to eight)

Materials/Preparation
- A piece of plain white paper for each participant
- A pen or pencil for each participant

Directions
1. Give everyone paper and a pen or pencil. Ask participants to
   make a small circle in the center of their pieces of paper. Tell
   them to label their circles "me."
2. Instruct them to draw another circle around the "me" circle,
   allowing about an inch of space between them. They should
   then draw another circle around the second circle, again leaving
   about an inch of distance between circles. They should continue
   this activity until they have filled up the paper with their circles.
3. Instruct participants that they are to place the people in their
   lives in the circle that best indicates how close they are to each
   person.
4. Tell participants that they should include anyone they have
   contact with in their everyday lives.
5. After they have completed their circles, ask them to share
   with their small groups any insights they had about their
   relationships at the workplace.

   Note: Different cultures define personal space very differently.
   Doing this activity with a very diverse group will lead to some
   lively discussion.

Processing the Activity

- Ask for volunteers to share their insights with the whole group.
- Ask participants if there is an appropriate circle in which to list co-workers.
- Ask what can happen if co-workers are in the "inner circles."

Trainer/Facilitator Insights

_____

_____

_____

_____

_____

_____

_____

_____

➤ Risky Business

Purpose   This activity gives participants the opportunity to talk about the risks they are willing and unwilling to take in their lives.

Risk Level   Moderate

Time   40 minutes

Number of Participants   Forty (small groups of six to eight)

Materials/Preparation   None

Directions
1. Tell participants that everyone has a different perception of what it means to take a risk. For one person it may be saying no to requests from others and for another it may be climbing a mountain. In fact, for some it may be both those things.
2. Instruct participants to share in their small groups some actions they consider to be risky.
3. Explain they can talk about physical risks, emotional risks, or both.
4. Ask each group to share the range of activities and behaviors that their group members considered risky.

Processing the Activity
- Ask participants what impact the differences in risk-taking behavior can have on a workplace team or group.
- Ask groups whether the sharing in their groups was more about emotional or physical risks.

Trainer/Facilitator Insights

_____

_____

_____

_____

_____

_____

_____

_____

➤ Stress, Stress, Stress

Purpose   This activity allows participants to think about realistic and funny ways to reduce stress in the workplace.

Risk Level   Low

Time   20 minutes

Number of Participants   Thirty (small groups of five to six)

Materials/Preparation
- Two pieces of flip chart paper for each small group
- Markers for each small group

Directions
1. Ask participants to form small groups. Distribute supplies, and then ask how many of them have stress in their workplace.

   Note: If the training is not related to the workplace, ask them about stress in their lives.

2. Instruct them to brainstorm in their small groups and list the kinds of stress they experience on a piece of chart paper. Ask them not to use names of people who cause them stress.
3. Tell participants to number the ideas on their lists.
4. Give each small group another piece of chart paper. Ask them to brainstorm both real and funny solutions to their stress issues. They should use the number that corresponds with the issue to identify solutions. Give an example: "If the number 1 stress issue is 'unrealistic deadlines,' the number 1 solution might be 'renegotiating the deadlines' or 'wearing a Superman suit to work the day after the assignment.'"
5. Ask each group to report to the other groups, sharing each stress issue and the solutions they brainstormed.

Processing the Activity

- Ask participants which kind of solution, realistic or funny, was easier to come up with and why.
- Ask what barriers exist that make it difficult to implement ideas to manage stress.

Trainer/Facilitator Insights

_____

_____

_____

_____

_____

_____

_____

_____

➔ What Do You See?

Purpose   This activity allows the group to explore the concept of perspective.

Risk Level   Low

Time   20 minutes

Number of Participants   Unlimited (small groups of six to eight)

Materials/Preparation
- Objects that have a distinct front and back, one object per small group, such as small clocks, paperback books, boxes of cereal or cake mix, and stuffed animals or dolls that can sit upright
- Napkins or paper bags
- A table for each small group

  Note: The objects do not all have to be different for each small group.

Directions
1. Cover each object with a napkin or paper bag before beginning.
2. Instruct small groups to divide themselves so that half the group is on one side of their table and half is on the other side.
3. Place a covered object in the center of each group's table so that the back of the object faces one part of the group and the front faces the other.
4. Instruct the groups to remove the covers from their objects and observe them. Participants may not stand or in any way attempt to see what is out of their line of vision. Allow about 1 minute for groups to observe, then cover the items again.
5. Tell participants to individually describe what they observed to their small groups.
6. Ask for volunteers from each small group to share some of the examples of differences in perspective that they experienced at their tables.

7. Ask for volunteers to share what they think influenced the different perspectives in their small groups.
8. Ask participants why there were differences in perspective, even among people observing the same thing.

Processing the Activity

• Ask participants how differences in perspective affect their work experiences.

Trainer/Facilitator Insights

_____

_____

_____

_____

_____

_____

_____

_____

➤ Whoops!

Purpose   This activity is designed to help participants to acknowledge that all people experience embarrassing situations in the workplace and that most of these have no enduring consequences.

Risk Level   Moderate

Time   20 minutes

Number of Participants   Unlimited (small groups of eight to ten)

Materials/Preparation   None

Directions
1. Within their small groups, ask participants to share the most embarrassing thing that has happened to them in a work situation. Tell them they can share a co-worker's situation (without giving the co-worker's name) if they can't think of one of their own.
2. Allow 15 minutes for sharing.
3. Ask for a volunteer from each group to share the most remarkable incident heard in the group.

Processing the Activity
- Ask participants how these incidents are similar.
- Ask participants how it felt to share their embarrassing moments.
- Ask whether any of the participants experienced repercussions from their embarrassing moments.

Note: The incidents usually seem funny in retrospect. They are usually the result of unplanned actions or circumstances. Most people have had these experiences.

Trainer/Facilitator Insights

_____

_____

_____

_____

_____

_____

_____

❯ Section 3
Norming

By the time groups reach the Norming stage, group members have settled down. Characteristically, participants' interactions are more personal and friendly. They are beginning to laugh more and to speak out. At this point they know each other and have resolved many of the issues they brought with them. Now the team must learn to work effectively together in this next step in group development.

Working as Teams

This section offers activities that encourage groups to practice teamwork. Team or group members have a more powerful learning experience than do individuals. Participants enhance one another's learning by sharing their ideas and insights. From the trainer's perspective, much more material can be covered in small teams and groups than if participants are working independently. The trainer or facilitator can divide assignments so that each group is working on a different part of the material. The groups then share their work with the rest of the participants. If this work is done by individuals, much more time is spent working through the assignment and processing the results.

Practicing working as a team helps groups to learn the strengths of group members. Leaders emerge during this process, as do people who are good summarizers, idea generators, writers, and facilitators. This process builds trust, as participants experience acceptance by the group for their contributions and ideas. The activities in this section are fun, nonthreatening ways to develop those relationships that create effective working teams.

Energizing Groups

Activities to energize groups are also found in this section. Energizers are defined as activities that renew people's energy. No matter how well groups are getting along, or how much they are accomplishing, they need occasional breaks from the training. Most trainers schedule one break in the morning and one in the afternoon. These time-outs are usually 15- or 20-minute intervals, with additional time used up getting people back into their seats. Rather than allowing additional, unstructured breaks during the day, facilitators can use brief and controlled energizers. The energizers simply change the focus of the participants for a short period of time, giving them the opportunity to stretch, share, and play a little. Participants are still in place and the trainer can return to the material and information quickly and easily. Energizers can be used at any time during a training or meeting.

Common Issues in Training and Group Work

What if . . .

- *A dominating leader emerges from the group?* When this happens, it sometimes pushes the group back to the Storming stage. Team members who were beginning to take on roles back off, and others become frustrated and angry about their lack of influence on the team. Trainers and facilitators need to intervene in these situations and state what they are observing to the whole group. For example, "It seems that very few team members are participating in this discussion. Is there something the team needs to do to get more even participation?" Another approach is to ask the team what is working well and what is not working for them. If the problem is not resolved with this approach, the trainer may need to speak to the dominator privately.

- *The comfort level of some team members triggers the sharing of inappropriate information (dirty jokes or very personal information)?* Stop the group's interaction. Explain that they are off the subject and that their sharing is inappropriate to the training. Bring the group's focus back to the work of the training by asking a question or giving an instruction.

- *Someone from a group leaves before the training is over?* A group member leaving before the training ends changes the dynamics of the group. Encourage them to discuss what the loss of a team member means to the group and how they will reapportion the work that the absent team member was doing.

- *Someone in a group is still uninvolved with the group, in spite of the team's efforts to include him/her?* At this point, you can tell the whole team to proceed with their work, whether or not everyone is willing to be involved. Making that statement often sends all eyes to the distant team member and prods him or her forward. If that doesn't happen, the team has been given permission to cease their efforts to involve that member and get on with their work.

- *Teams become competitive where competition was not the intended purpose of an activity?* Teams often do become competitive in a good-natured way. If the competition becomes too serious, it can interfere with learning. Monitor the level of competition and keep teams focused on the work of the training.

- *Someone protests that an activity or energizer is "silly" or "a waste of time"?* Give the protester the option of not participating and quickly continue with the activity. If you give the protester too much attention, others may pick up on the negative attitude.

Energizers

Agree or Disagree

Alphabet Angst

Hee Haw

Musical Pictures

Oh Wow!

Orchestrate

Pop-Up

Start Talking

Storycise

Take It Easy

Taking Care of Ourselves

Talent Share

A Walk in the Park

➤ Agree or Disagree

Purpose   This activity is intended to energize the participants. It can be used any time during the training.

Risk Level   Moderate

Time   10 minutes

Number of Participants   Unlimited

Materials/Preparation
- A copy of the Agree-or-Disagree Statements sheet for the facilitator

Directions
1. Tell participants that you will be reading statements. If they agree with the statements, they should move to left side of the room (point to the left side). If they disagree with the statements, they should move to the right side of the room (point to the right). If they are undecided, they should stand in the middle of the room.
2. Read each statement and tell participants to move to the left side of the room if they agree, the right if they disagree, or the middle if they are undecided.
3. Ask for volunteers from each area of the room to share why they chose to stand where they did.
4. Continue the activity, reading a statement and giving participants the opportunity to move. Be sure to ask for volunteers to explain their choices each time they move.

Processing the Activity
- Ask participants what differences of opinion do for a discussion.
- Ask whether it was it hard for participants to defend their positions on some of the statements.

Trainer/Facilitator Insights

_____

_____

_____

_____

_____

_____

_____

_____

Agree-or-Disagree Statements

Technology has improved the world.

Dancing is the best form of exercise.

Pizza is good for you.

A dog is man's or woman's best friend.

Mountain climbing is not really scary.

➤ Alphabet Angst

Purpose   This energizer helps participants take a break from the work of the training.

Risk Level   Low

Time   10 minutes

Number of Participants   Unlimited

Materials/Preparation
- Copies of the Alphabet Angst Puzzle Sheet, one per participant
- A pencil for each participant
- Small prizes

Directions
1. Tell participants that they will have 10 minutes to find the answer to the puzzle. Hand out the Puzzle Sheets.
2. Ask them to raise their hands as soon as they have the solution, but not to share their answer with anyone else.
3. Call time at the end of 10 minutes.
4. Give a prize to the first one or two people who raised their hands and answered correctly.
5. Tell participants that the answer is Park Bench, which is the word that is left when you remove the letters that spell Five Letters.

Processing the Activity
- Ask participants if anyone has had an experience like this before, where instructions or explanations had a double meaning.
- Tell participants it is time to get back to the work of the training.

Trainer/Facilitator Insights

_____

_____

_____

_____

_____

_____

_____

Alphabet Angst Puzzle Sheet

Instructions: Take out five letters and find something found in most cities.

F P I A R V K E L B E E N T C T E H R S

➤ Hee Haw

Purpose   This activity is used to quickly energize a group.

Risk Level   Low to Moderate

Time   5 minutes

Number of Participants   Forty maximum

Materials/Preparation   None

Space Requirements   Enough open space to fit a circle of all participants

Directions
1. Ask participants to form one big circle.
2. Tell them you will start a laugh that you will pass to the person on your left. That person will laugh and pass it on until the laugh has gone all the way around the circle.
3. Explain that you will keep the laugh going until someone in the circle is really laughing.

   Note: Someone is always really laughing by the second time around.

Processing the Activity
- Ask participants whether they notice a change in the energy in the room. Invite someone to describe the change.
- Ask participants how laughing affects them. (Laughter releases tension. People are often more relaxed after a good laugh.)

Trainer/Facilitator Insights

_____

_____

_____

_____

_____

_____

_____

_____

➤ Musical Pictures

Purpose   This activity offers participants a short break.

Risk Level   Low

Time   10 minutes

Number of Participants   Unlimited

Materials/Preparation
- Plain paper, 8½ × 11 or larger, one piece for each participant
- Assorted markers or crayons
- A CD player
- A classical, meditative, or easy-listening CD

Directions
1. Distribute paper and markers.
2. Tell participants that they will be listening to music and should draw or use colors to show what the music evokes in them.
3. Play the music for 5 minutes.
4. Ask for volunteers to share their drawings with the group.

Processing the Activity
- Ask participants how music can set a mood.
- Ask participants whether they use music to unwind or relax.
- Ask volunteers to share the kind of music they use to relax.

Trainer/Facilitator Insights

_____

_____

_____

_____

_____

_____

_____

➤ Oh Wow!

Purpose This activity is a brief energizer, to be used at any time during the training.

Risk Level Moderate

Time 10 minutes at the beginning, in 3-minute bursts during the training, and 10 minutes to process at the end of training

Number of Participants Unlimited

Materials/Preparation None

Directions

1. Ask participants to think of an "Oh Wow!" experience they might like to share with the whole group. Give them an example of an "Oh Wow!" experience you have had.

   Note: If participants have had some experience with the subject of the training, they can share "Oh Wow!" moments related to the subject of the training. If the training material is new to them, ask participants to share from their personal or professional lives. A personal "Oh Wow!" experience might be viewing an especially beautiful sunset or crossing the finish line of a challenging road race.

2. Explain that you will be calling for people to share at different times throughout the training. Ask participants to limit their sharing to 3 minutes.

   Note: People often get bogged down in their everyday lives. "Oh Wow!" experiences remind us that life can be dramatic and exciting.

Processing the Activity

- At the end of the training, ask participants why this kind of sharing can be energizing.
- Ask whether or not others were reminded of their own "Oh Wow!" experiences when listening to others share. Invite a few more to share.

Trainer/Facilitator Insights

_____

_____

_____

_____

_____

_____

_____

_____

➤ Orchestrate

Purpose   This activity energizes participants in a creative way.

Risk Level   Low to Moderate

Time   20 minutes

Number of Participants   Forty maximum

Materials/Preparation   None

Directions
1. Tell the group that they are about to become an orchestra.
2. Instruct participants to form eight equal-size groups.
3. Assign each group to be an instrument as follows: violin, trombone, drum, bass, clarinet, flute, piano, and harp.
4. Tell each group to practice making a sound similar to the sound of their assigned instrument.
5. Ask the groups to move together, with the piano group seated in the middle front, the harp group seated to one side, and the drum group seated on the other. The other instrument groups should stand behind the seated groups.
6. Explain that you will lead the orchestra in the classic song "Row, Row, Row Your Boat."
7. Tell them to start when you nod. Allow the orchestra one practice before the final "performance."
8. Applaud the group and tell them they make beautiful music together.

Processing the Activity

- Ask whether anyone in the group plays an instrument.
- Invite participants to share what instruments they play.

Trainer/Facilitator Insights

_____

_____

_____

_____

_____

_____

_____

_____

➤ Pop-Up

Purpose   This activity is an energizer that should be used at a mid-point in the training.

Risk Level   Moderate

Time   5 minutes

Number of Participants   Thirty maximum

Materials/Preparation   None

Directions

1. Tell participants that they have had some time to get to know their teammates or many of the group members.
2. Explain that you will start the activity by pointing at a participant and calling out something you know or think about that participant. That participant then stands and points to someone else and calls out something he or she knows or thinks about that participant. No negative comments are permitted. For example: You might know a participant was born in Boston, so you would point to him or her and call out, "Born in Boston."
3. Tell participants to call out something positive about a person's smile or shoes (anything nonthreatening) if they don't remember anything else.
4. Continue this activity until everyone is standing.

Processing the Activity

- Ask participants what is easiest to remember about others.
- Invite everyone to sit down again and get back to the training.

Trainer/Facilitator Insights

_____

_____

_____

_____

_____

_____

_____

_____

➤ Start Talking

Purpose   This activity is designed to allow participants to become energized and have fun.

Risk Level   Low

Time   15 minutes

Number of Participants   Unlimited (small groups of six or eight)

Materials/Preparation   None

Directions
1. Form small groups of six to eight. Tell participants to identify someone creative in their small group.
2. Explain that this person will start a story. Any theme is acceptable.
3. After 2 minutes, call time and say that the person to the left of the speaker must continue the story.
4. Again, after 2 minutes, call time and say that the person to the speaker's left continues the story.
5. When the story gets to the person to the right of the first speaker, say that he or she must provide the ending to the story.
6. Ask one person from each group to summarize the group's story.

Processing the Activity
- Ask participants why this kind of activity is energizing (because it is fun and focuses on something other than the work of the training).
- Invite participants to return to the training.

Trainer/Facilitator Insights

_____

_____

_____

_____

_____

_____

_____

➤ Storycise

Purpose   This activity is a quick energizer.

Risk Level   Low

Time   5 minutes

Number of Participants   Unlimited

Materials/Preparation
- A copy of the Storycise: Read-Aloud Story for the facilitator

Directions
1. Tell participants that you will be reading a story and they are to do the actions described in the story without leaving their seats.
2. Read the story, acting out each movement along with participants.

Processing the Activity
- Ask participants what the benefits are to taking short breaks involving physical activity.

Trainer/Facilitator Insights

_____

_____

_____

_____

_____

_____

_____

Storycise: Read-Aloud Story

Izzy the Imp lived with his family in a small square space with very high walls. All of his family were very little, but Izzy was growing bigger every day. First his right leg stretched out. *(Stretch out right leg.)* He could barely see his feet as he wiggled his toes. *(Wiggle toes.)* Then his left leg stretched out. *(Stretch out left leg.)* Sure enough, he could not see his left foot as he wiggled his toes. *(Wiggle toes.)* He even leaned over to try to touch his toes *(lean over and touch toes)*, but it was no use. Izzy's family decided he should go out into the land of big people, as they were running out of room for him in their small space. So they put a ladder against the wall and Izzy pulled himself up the ladder one rung at a time *(move arms up and down as if climbing a ladder)*. At the top Izzy peered over the wall and tilted his head to the left and then the right, and then he did it again *(tilt head both ways twice)*. He seemed to like what he saw, because he waved with his right hand *(wave with right hand)* and he waved with his left hand *(wave with left hand)* and then he waved with both hands *(wave with both hands)*. Then suddenly he disappeared over the wall. Later, his family received a message that he had met Ingrid Imp, who also grew too much, and they were living in a much larger space happily ever after. The End

⊒ Take It Easy

Purpose   This activity offers participants a short break from
the training.

Risk Level   Low

Time   5 minutes

Number of Participants   Unlimited

Materials/Preparation
- A CD player
- Soothing music

Directions
1. Tell participants that you will be turning on music and dimming
   the lights for 5 minutes.
2. Explain that while the music is on they can stretch, relax, or get
   up and move around.

Processing the Activity
- Ask participants to return to the work of the training.

Trainer/Facilitator Insights

_____

_____

_____

_____

_____

_____

_____

➤ Taking Care of Ourselves

Purpose   This activity is intended to give participants an energizing break.

Risk Level   Moderate

Time   20 minutes

Number of Participants   Unlimited

Materials/Preparation   None

Space Requirements   Enough space to allow movement of the whole group at one time

Directions
1. Ask for three volunteers who are willing to share an activity they do for fun or to stay healthy.
2. Tell them they will be demonstrating what they do and leading participants in the activity (dancing, aerobics, stretching, weightlifting using books, singing, walking, jogging).
3. Give each volunteer 5 minutes for his or her activity.
4. Applaud the volunteers.

Processing the Activity
- Ask participants what else people do to handle stress and stay healthy.
- Tell participants it is time to return to the work of the training.

Trainer/Facilitator Insights

_____

_____

_____

_____

_____

_____

_____

_____

➤ Talent Share

Purpose   This activity invites participants to arrive at the training prepared to share a talent. The training should be longer than two days to give participants the opportunity to present their talents.

Risk Level   Moderate to High

Time   3 minutes per talent

Number of Participants   Ten to fifteen

Materials/Preparation
- Include in the registration information mailed to participants an invitation for people who have a talent they would like to share to bring their instruments, crafts, or whatever with them to the training.
- Have a sign-up sheet at the registration desk at the training where the participants can list what talents they plan to share.

Directions
1. Tell participants that during breaks and at lunch they will have the opportunity to be entertained by fellow participants.
2. Scatter the entertainment throughout the day, saving particularly upbeat, funny, or energetic sharing for the afternoons and ends of training days.
3. Be sure to introduce all performers and to applaud all efforts.

   Note: If this is a large training, limit the sharing to the first ten or fifteen people who sign up, and include that information in the letter.

Processing the Activity

- At the close of the training thank performers again.
- Tell participants how amazing it is to realize how many talented people there are in this world.

Trainer/Facilitator Insights

_____

_____

_____

_____

_____

_____

_____

⊐ A Walk in the Park

Purpose   This activity allows participants the opportunity to share a positive experience with others.

Risk Level   Low

Time   35 minutes

Number of Participants   Twenty

Materials/Preparation
- Access to the outdoors and good weather

Directions
1. Tell participants to spend 10 minutes outside seeking inspiration from nature. Explain that they should not talk during this time, but simply reflect on their surroundings.
2. When participants return, form small groups and instruct them to share within their group any inspiration they had during their sojourn with nature.

Processing the Activity
- Ask participants why the out-of-doors is thought to be inspiring.
- Ask volunteers to share other life experiences that were inspiring to them.

Trainer/Facilitator Insights

_____

_____

_____

_____

_____

_____

Team Building

At the Races

Bag Ball

Getting Down to Business

The Greatest Team on Earth

Like a Rock

Making Changes

The Neighborhood

On First

Perfect Retirement

Reaching Consensus

Scrabble on the Run

Sing, Sing, Sing!

Task and Process

Tasty Teams

Team Sculpture

Two Sides to the Story

We'll Be Back in a Moment

What Would You Do?

Where Are We?

➤ At the Races

Purpose   This activity gives participants the opportunity to practice working in teams.

Risk Level   Low

Time   30 minutes

Number of Participants   Fifty maximum (small groups of six to eight).

Materials/Preparation
- Small toy race cars, one per team
- Chart paper with columns titled as follows: Car Model, Driver Name, Sponsor, Logo
- A marker
- Space on floor marked with a starting line with chalk or masking tape
- A ribbon or other first-place award

Directions
1. Form small groups and distribute a race car to each team.
2. Instruct teams to work together to come up with logos for their cars, names for the drivers, and a sponsor.
3. Once they have made those decisions, ask them to send someone to the chart to record that information.
4. Announce the race and ask contestants to line up at the starting line.
5. Explain that when you say "go," contestants should push their cars as far as the starting line and then let go. The car that travels the farthest wins.
6. Present the ribbon or award to the winning team.

Processing the Activity

• Ask teams how they made decisions in their groups.

Trainer/Facilitator Insights

_____

_____

_____

_____

_____

_____

_____

_____

➤ Bag Ball

Purpose   This activity is a lively way of doing team building.

Risk Level   Low to Moderate

Time   20 minutes

Number of Participants   Forty maximum (small groups of six to eight)

Materials/Preparation
- Open space
- Two large paper bags per team
- Five or six tennis balls per team
- Several balls of string
- Small prizes or candy for the winning team

Directions
1. Form teams and ask them to find a place in the room to form lines.
2. Place a paper bag containing five or six tennis balls at one end of each team's line. Place the second, empty paper bag at the other end of each line.
3. Explain that the teams will be handing tennis balls down their lines as quickly as possible.
4. Tell them each person must receive and pass on each tennis ball. The last person in the line will put the ball in the paper bag. If a team member drops the ball it must be put in the starting bag and be passed again.
5. Tell them they will do this activity with their hands tied together at the wrist with string (the back of one person's right hand tied to the back of the next person's left hand). Participants on either end of the lines will have an outside hand free.
6. Instruct teams to tie the hands of another team and continue until there is only one team not tied. Tie that team's hands yourself.

7. Check to make sure everyone understands that they are to pass the balls, hand to hand, all the way down the line. Remind them that if they drop a ball they must start over with that ball.
8. Say "go."
9. Award a prize or candy to the members of the winning team.

Processing the Activity
- Ask teams what they had to do to accomplish the task.
- Ask participants how they demonstrated good teamwork.

Trainer/Facilitator Insights

_____

_____

_____

_____

_____

_____

_____

_____

➤ Getting Down to Business

Purpose   This activity gives teams the opportunity to identify skills of team members.

Risk Level   Moderate

Time   30 minutes

Number of Participants   Thirty (small groups of five or six)

Materials/Preparation   None

Directions

1. Have everyone form into small groups and tell participants that they will be assessing the skills of their team members.
2. Explain that they will choose a business based on these skills and interests. For example, one team member may be a good cook and a skilled decorator. Another may have a background in sales and an interest in writing. Other members may include a bookkeeper and manager who also has an interest in cooking. The business this team chooses could be a restaurant.
3. Once the team has decided on a business appropriate for their team members' skills and interests, ask them to identify the job each team member would have in the business.
4. Invite each team to share its work with the whole group.

Processing the Activity

- Ask participants what they learned from this activity.
- Ask how they can apply this learning to their workplaces.

Trainer/Facilitator Insights

_____

_____

_____

_____

_____

_____

_____

_____

➤ The Greatest Team on Earth

Purpose   This activity is designed to start participants thinking about the qualities of good team members.

Risk Level   Low

Time   20 minutes

Number of Participants   Thirty (small groups of five or six)

Materials/Preparation
- Flip chart paper for each group
- Assorted markers
- Masking tape or push pins

Directions
1. Form participants into small groups. Tell participants they will be working within their groups to design a great team member.
2. Explain that they will draw a large representation of a person on the chart paper. (They can draw stick figures.)
3. Instruct the group to add internal and external body parts that represent characteristics of a good team member. For example, ears could represent a good listener, and a heart could represent caring or compassion.
4. Groups should post their drawings on the training room walls once they are complete.

   Note: This activity can get a little silly. You may want to ask that reproductive body parts not be included as part of the drawings.

Processing the Activity

- Ask each group to share their design of a "great team member."
- Note the universal characteristics included in the different drawings.
- Note the unique ideas of some groups.

Trainer/Facilitator Insights

_____

_____

_____

_____

_____

_____

_____

_____

➤ Like a Rock

Purpose   This activity encourages creative teamwork.

Risk Level   Low

Time   25 minutes

Number of Participants   Unlimited (small groups of six to eight)

Materials/Preparation
- Art supplies such as glue, colored paper, scissors, ribbon/string, fabric, and so on
- Rocks about the size of a tennis ball, one per small group

Directions
1. Display art supplies at the front of the room. Ask participants to form small groups and then distribute rocks, one per small group.
2. Tell participants to work within their groups to convert their rocks to something else.
3. Instruct them to come to an agreement on what they want their rocks to be and then work together to create the transformation.
4. Ask each group to share their creation with the whole group.

Processing the Activity
- Ask teams what process they used to make their decisions.
- Ask them how they ensured that the work on their rock was a team effort.

Trainer/Facilitator Insights

_____

_____

_____

_____

_____

_____

_____

_____

➤ Making Changes

Purpose   This activity helps participants to explore the concept of change.

Risk Level   Moderate

Time   20 minutes

Number of Participants   Unlimited (small groups of six to eight)

Materials/Preparation
- The following posted on a piece of flip chart paper or an overhead transparency: Stages of Change—Resistance, Acknowledgment, Exploration, Experimentation, Commitment
- Paper and a pencil for each participant

Directions
1. Explain the stages of changes as follows: "Change is a natural part of life. However, human beings resist change, even when the change is to their benefit. When we consider change, we begin the process by acknowledging the necessity of it. We begin to explore the possibilities of change and even experiment with the change. It is, however, our commitment to change that actually makes it happen."
2. Ask participants to form small groups and to think about small or major changes they have made in their lives.
3. Distribute paper and pencils. Tell them to write down the steps they took toward making the change.
4. Instruct them to share what they wrote in their small groups.

Note: You may want to share a change you made as an example.

Processing the Activity

- Ask for volunteers to talk about a change they made and the steps they took to make it.
- Explain that they will be making small or large changes in their work/lives with the new information/skills they gain from the training.

Trainer/Facilitator Insights

_____

_____

_____

_____

_____

_____

_____

_____

➤ The Neighborhood

Purpose   This activity allows participants to practice working as
    teams.

Risk Level   Low

Time   25 minutes

Number of Participants   Unlimited (small groups of five or six)

Materials/Preparation
- Copies of The Neighborhood: Story Lines with sentences cut into
  individual strips. There should be a set of story strips for each
  group.

Directions
1. Ask participants to form small groups. Give each small group a
   set of story strips and instruct them to divide the strips among
   group members.
2. Tell them it is each group's job to put the sentence strips in
   order.
3. Explain that each participant must place his or her own strips,
   but that other team members can make suggestions.
4. Allow groups 10 minutes to put their story strips in order.
5. Ask the first team finished to read their story aloud.

Processing the Activity
- Ask the teams what they had to do to accomplish this task.
- Ask participants if it would have been easier or more difficult to
  do this task individually. Why or why not?

Trainer/Facilitator Insights

_____

_____

_____

_____

_____

_____

_____

_____

The Neighborhood: Story Lines

The Higgenses and the Ellingsworths were neighbors.

Even though they lived side by side, they did not speak to each other.

It all started when Chester Ellingsworth won the lottery.

He decided to take a trip around the world.

Because he would be away for a long time, Chester broke his engagement to Wilma Higgens.

Wilma and her father, Walter, sued Chester for breach of contract.

Chester countersued, claiming that Wilma owed him money.

Chester lost his suit.

The Higgenses won theirs.

Chester had to give them half his winnings from the lottery.

He was furious about his loss and swore he would get revenge.

To spite the Higgenses, Chester asked another neighbor, Geraldine Jones, to marry him.

Geraldine said yes.

On the day of the wedding, Wilma swallowed her pride and went to see Chester.

She wished him well in his marriage to Geraldine.

As Chester stood listening to Wilma's kind words, he realized he still loved her.

He told Wilma how he was feeling and asked her to marry him.

Wilma said yes.

Chester married Wilma that day.

Geraldine and her father, James, sued Chester for breach of promise.

Now the Joneses and the Ellingsworths do not speak, even though they are neighbors.

⊒ On First

Purpose   This activity gives participants the opportunity to explore teamwork by looking at team sports.

Risk Level   Low

Time   30 minutes

Number of Participants   Forty (small groups of six to eight)

Materials/Preparation
- Flip chart paper and a marker for each group

Directions
1. Form small groups of six to eight people and give each group flip chart paper and a marker.
2. Tell participants that developing groups that work effectively together is similar to developing a sports team. For example, think about bringing together a group of people who are interested in playing softball. What do they have to do to create a successful ball team?
3. Instruct groups to choose a team sport they are familiar with and list the process they must go through to build a successful team. Tell them to list the steps for developing their team on the right side of a piece of flip chart paper.
4. Once they have completed that list, they should list the steps for building an effective work group on the left side of the paper.
5. Ask each group to share their lists.

Processing the Activity

- Ask participants to identify similarities in the two lists.
- Ask for volunteers to note differences in the sports team and work group lists.
- Ask for volunteers to share how they think the effectiveness or lack of effectiveness in work groups affects attitudes toward work.

Trainer/Facilitator Insights

_____

_____

_____

_____

_____

_____

_____

_____

➤ Perfect Retirement

Purpose   This activity allows participants to work in groups to describe the perfect retirement.

Risk Level   Low to Moderate

Time   15 minutes

Number of Participants   Forty maximum

Materials/Preparation
- Paper and a pencil for each group

Directions
1. Ask participants to form small groups. Give each group paper and a pencil.
2. Tell them that their group will be retiring soon and that they are to come up with the perfect retirement for the group, including as much detail as possible. Have one member of each group compile the plan as other members contribute ideas.
3. Give them 5 minutes to complete their task.
4. Invite each group to quickly share its retirement plans.

Processing the Activity
- Ask participants how they made decisions.
- Ask groups how difficult it was for them to agree on a plan so quickly.

Trainer/Facilitator Insights

_____

_____

_____

_____

_____

_____

⊇ Reaching Consensus

Purpose   This activity offers participants the opportunity to practice reaching consensus.

Note: Consensus is a way of reaching agreement that allows all members of the decision-making group to have a voice. Group members must agree that they can support the decision of the group, whether or not they are in complete accord with the rest of the group. If a participant cannot agree to support the decision, the group must go "back to the drawing board" until they can make a decision that has unanimous support from the members.

Risk Level   Moderate

Time   40 minutes

Number of Participants   Unlimited (small groups of four to six)

Materials/Preparation
- One copy of the Reaching Consensus Fact Sheet for each participant
- A pen or pencil for each participant

Directions
1. After participants form small groups, tell them that they will be choosing one famous person to invite to a dinner with the group. The person can be famous or infamous, alive or dead.

   Note: The person chosen should not be a religious figure.

2. Explain that the group must come to consensus on who that famous person will be. Explain what consensus means.
3. Distribute the Reaching Consensus Fact Sheet.

4. Explain that participants should work alone to list a few people they might want to invite on the top of the Fact Sheet. They should list some characteristics of those people that they find interesting.
5. Once they have completed their Fact Sheets, they should work as a group to select one person from all the lists.
6. Remind participants that this is not a vote, but rather an agreement that includes the entire group.
7. Once they have completed the process, invite each group to share its choice.

Processing the Activity

- Ask participants why consensus is often used to reach agreement instead of voting. (In consensus, no one loses as people do in voting.)
- Ask for volunteers to share how their groups went about reaching consensus.

Trainer/Facilitator Insights

_____

_____

_____

_____

_____

_____

_____

_____

Reaching Consensus Fact Sheet

Famous people I might wish to invite to dinner:

1.

2.

3.

Characteristics of these people I find interesting:

Person 1:

Person 2:

Person 3:

➤ Scrabble on the Run

Purpose   This activity is a fast-moving way for participants to describe their teams.

Risk Level   Low

Time   10 minutes

Number of Participants   Unlimited (small groups of six to eight)

Materials/Preparation
- Individual cards depicting letters of the alphabet. Have two or more sets of alphabet cards (depending on the size of the group).
- Candy or other small prizes.

Directions
1. Form groups. Distribute six alphabet cards face down to each small group. Lay the rest of the cards on a table in front of the room face down.
2. Tell groups that they will try to make as many words describing their teams as is possible in 5 minutes.
3. Explain that there are additional alphabet cards at the front of the room that they can pick up and take back to their teams. They are to take no more than three cards at a time from the front table and must return one at the same time.
4. Tell them that when you say "go" they can turn their cards over and begin. When you call "time," they should stop immediately.
5. At the end of 5 minutes, ask each group to share the words they came up with to describe their team.
6. Declare one or more winners and distribute prizes.

Processing the Activity

- Ask groups to share how they worked together as teams.
- Ask how competition changes the way individuals on teams behave.

Trainer/Facilitator Insights

_____

_____

_____

_____

_____

_____

_____

_____

➤ Sing, Sing, Sing!

Purpose   This activity allows participants to practice working together toward a common goal.

Risk Level   Moderate

Time   15 to 20 minutes (depending on the size of the group)

Number of Participants   Unlimited

Materials/Preparation
- Strips of paper with the lines of "America the Beautiful" (see Sample Song Sheet), or another song familiar to the group, written on them, one line per slip. (The song can be divided into eight lines.) Make enough duplicates for each line so that small groups of participants will be singing the same part of the song. For example, with forty participants in five groups of eight, five people will have the same part to sing.

  Note: "America the Beautiful" is the example we use here as a song that is familiar to most Americans. Choose any song that is suited for and familiar to the group.

Directions
1. Distribute the slips of paper, one per participant.
2. Instruct participants to move around the room singing their lines until they find others with the same part of the song.
3. The whole group should then put themselves in the order of the song, with "Oh beautiful for spacious skies" as the first line, and so on.
4. Once the group is in order, ask them to sing the song all the way through.

Processing the Activity

- Ask what might have happened if the group had not worked together.
- Ask whether there are tasks that require cooperative effort in the workplace. Ask for an example from a participant's experience.

Trainer/Facilitator Insights

_____

_____

_____

_____

_____

_____

_____

_____

Sing, Sing, Sing: Sample Song Sheet

Line 1: *Oh beautiful for spacious skies*

Line 2: *For amber waves of grain*

Line 3: *For purple mountains' majesty*

Line 4: *Above a fruited plain*

Line 5: *America, America, God shed His grace on thee*

Line 6: *And crown thy good*

Line 7: *With brotherhood*

Line 8: *From sea to shining sea*

➤ Task and Process

Purpose   This activity involves participants in a task related to the training and requires them to pay attention to how their team works together.

Risk Level   Moderate to High

Time   40 minutes

Number of Participants   Unlimited (small groups of six to eight)

Materials/Preparation
- Any assignment from the training material that requires group work

Directions
1. Give an assignment that participants can work on within their small groups. The assignment should be from the training material.
2. Tell groups that they are to work on this task, but also notice the way that the members of each group work together. Each participant should make a few notes about how he or she sees the team going about its work. For example: Does someone seem to lead the group? Is everyone engaged in the work? Are some people more involved than others? Does someone facilitate the process rather than leading it?
3. Once the groups have completed their assignments, ask them to talk in their groups about how they perceived the process.
4. Ask each group to share with the larger group the new learning they gained from the assignment.
5. Ask groups to share with the larger group the discussion they had about their group process.

Processing the Activity

- Ask participants what they consider to be a good process for working together.
- Ask for volunteers to share what they felt they contributed to their group's process.

Trainer/Facilitator Insights

_____

_____

_____

_____

_____

_____

_____

_____

➤ Tasty Teams

Purpose　　This activity is a quick way for teams to evaluate their work together.

Risk Level　　Low

Time　　5 minutes

Number of Participants　　Unlimited (small groups of six to eight)

Materials/Preparation　　None

Directions

1. Ask small groups to discuss the kind of team they are and then to describe it as a food.
2. Give an example: "A team might choose to identify themselves as popcorn, because they are bursting with energy."
3. Ask each group what food they chose and why.

Processing the Activity

- Ask each team why they described themselves as they did.
- Ask how teams form personalities all their own.

Trainer/Facilitator Insights

_____

_____

_____

_____

_____

_____

_____

_____

➤ Team Sculpture

Purpose   This activity helps teams to look at how they work together.

Risk Level   Moderate

Time   25 minutes

Number of Participants   Thirty maximum (small groups of five or six)

Materials/Preparation   None

Directions
1. Tell participants that they will be using their bodies to create a sculpture that depicts the way their team works. The sculpture should include all team members.
2. Tell teams to discuss the way they think they work together as a team before creating the sculptures. For example, a team that has a dominant leader might have the leader standing and other team members sitting around the leader in a circle.
3. Each team should present to the whole group.
4. Applaud every effort.

Processing the Activity
- Ask if anyone would like to ask questions of one of the teams.
- Ask for volunteers from each team to explain what they learned about their team or their role on the team.
- Ask whether or not this information will change the way they do business in their group.

Trainer/Facilitator Insights

_____

_____

_____

_____

_____

_____

_____

_____

⊵ Two Sides to the Story

Purpose   This activity allows teams to look at a situation from two
different viewpoints.

Risk Level   Low to Moderate

Time   20 minutes

Number of Participants   Twenty maximum

Materials/Preparation
- A copy of the "Two Sides to the Story" handout for each
participant

Directions
1. Divide the participants into two groups.
2. Distribute the "Two Sides to the Story" handout.
3. Tell one group privately that they will be advocates for the boy
and the old man, arguing that Jane was wrong for cheating them.
4. Tell the other group privately that they will advocate for Jane and
her well-intentioned effort to save her family from starvation.
5. Explain that the groups will present arguments to the whole
group from their assigned perspectives.
6. Give each group 5 minutes to prepare its argument.
7. Ask each group to present the arguments they have developed.
8. Invite the whole group to vote according to the perspective they
actually support after listening to both sides.

Processing the Activity
- Was it hard to argue your side if you really didn't believe in it?
- Describe a time when you were asked to see something from
someone else's perspective.

Trainer/Facilitator Insights

_____

_____

_____

_____

_____

_____

_____

_____

Two Sides to the Story

A poor farmer lived at the edge of town. He could barely grow enough food to feed his family. One day, he called his oldest daughter to him and said, "Jane, winter is coming, and we do not have enough food to keep us alive until spring." He showed her an old pocket watch. "Take this old watch to town and trade it for a chicken and a sack of flour."

Jane started out for town. On the way, she met a peddler selling red and gold beads. "Look here, young woman," he said. "I have beautiful beads, worth a king's ransom, and I will sell them to you for just a few pennies."

"I have no money," said Jane. "All I have is this old watch. I am trading it for a chicken and a sack of flour."

"Ah," said the peddler. "Give me the watch, and I will give you enough beads to buy twenty chickens and twenty sacks of flour."

"How can I be sure these beads are worth that much?" Jane asked.

"Look," said the peddler. "See how they sparkle in the sun like diamonds."

Jane thought the beads were indeed beautiful and agreed to trade the watch for them.

When she arrived in town, her first stop was the general store. She put a few of the beads on the counter and said that she would like to buy some flour and a few chickens.

"Not with those beads, you won't," said the shopkeeper. "Those are nothing but pieces of glass."

Jane was bereft. She had been tricked, for sure. She sat on the curb, wondering what she could do to keep her family from starving.

Then she saw a young boy walking down the road, carrying two chickens. She ran up to him. "Young man," she said, "I have valuable beads that I will trade you for those chickens." She showed him the beads, making sure the sun shone on them and made them sparkle.

"Oh," said the boy, "they are beautiful. But I am supposed to take these chickens to my grandmother."

"You can use some of the beads to buy more chickens," Jane said, "and still have some left to buy candy."

The boy handed Jane the chickens, and Jane handed him half the beads in return.

Quickly, Jane ran to the grist mill. There was an old man filling sacks with flour. "Sir," Jane said, "I would like to trade these beads for two sacks of flour."

The old man squinted at the beads Jane held out. "My, my," he said, "they are pretty. But how do I know they are worth two sacks of flour?"

"Come into the sunshine, and I will show you," Jane said.

Sure enough, because of the way the beads sparkled in the sunshine, the old man thought they were diamonds. Soon Jane was on her way home with two chickens and two sacks of flour.

➤ We'll Be Back in a Moment

Purpose   This activity involves participants from the same organization in team building.

Risk Level   Low

Time   20 minutes

Number of Participants   Forty maximum (small groups of six to eight)

Materials/Preparation   None

Directions
1. Tell groups that they will be developing commercials about their workplace. The commercials should have a positive spin.
2. Explain that they will be presenting their commercials to the whole group.
3. Tell the groups that they have 5 minutes to prepare 1-minute commercials.
4. When groups present, applaud all efforts.

Processing the Activity
- Ask groups how they came to an agreement on the subject of their commercials.
- Ask how thinking positively about the workplace affects the atmosphere.

Trainer/Facilitator Insights

_____

_____

_____

_____

_____

_____

➤ What Would You Do?

Purpose   This activity offers participants the opportunity to practice working with issues that arise in the workplace.

Risk Level   High

Time   40 minutes

Number of Participants   Thirty maximum (small groups of six to eight)

Materials/Preparation
- Individual 8½ × 11 pieces of lined paper with a different issue from the What Would You Do? Issues List written at the top of each piece
- A pen or pencil for each group

   Note: You may increase or decrease the number of issues discussed, based on the number of small groups you are working with or the time you have allotted for this activity.

Directions
1. Distribute a different sheet to each group. Tell them to discuss the issue stated at the top of their paper and write their best answer down on the paper. Allow 5 minutes for their discussion.
2. Instruct the groups to pass their issue sheet to another group, working clockwise around the room.
3. Tell them to discuss the issue stated, as they did before, and write their best answer on the sheet. Continue this process until every group has had an opportunity to discuss each issue.

Processing the Activity
- Ask for each group to report to the others on the issue sheet they have at their table.
- Ask why, in some cases, there are many solutions to the same problem.
- Ask for volunteers to share their personal approaches to handling difficult issues with co-workers.

Trainer/Facilitator Insights

_____

_____

_____

_____

_____

_____

_____

_____

What Would You Do? Issues List

- Your co-worker shares that she has a serious illness. She did not ask you to keep the information confidential. As her impending absences may affect the business, should you tell your boss?

- The person working in the next cubicle has personal phone conversations throughout the day. You can clearly hear the non-work-related subjects of these conversations through the partition. How should you handle it?

- One of your co-workers signs up for a conference, picks up his name tag, and leaves. You notice that he is not in attendance at any of the sessions. How should you handle it?

- At a meeting, a co-worker takes credit for ideas generated by several of you. What should you do?

- A co-worker embarrasses his colleagues by not taking commitments seriously. He is late for meetings and does not bring material he is supposed to have prepared. It is especially embarrassing when meetings involve clients or guests. Management seems oblivious to this problem. What can you and your colleagues do?

⟩ Where Are We?

Purpose   This activity allows participants to practice working in teams.

Risk Level   Low

Time   20 minutes

Number of Participants   Thirty (small groups of five or six)

Materials/Preparation
  • The following settings written on individual slips of paper: Fire Station, Hospital, Restaurant, Police Station, School, Airport

Directions
  1. Form groups. Tell participants that there are many work settings where people must work in teams to accomplish their tasks.
  2. Explain that you will be handing out one slip of paper to each small group and that each slip has a different work setting written on it.
  3. Tell participants to work together to provide a demonstration of the kind of teamwork that would occur in that work setting. They should not reveal their assigned work settings to other groups.
  4. Allow groups 10 minutes to prepare their demonstrations.
  5. Ask each group to make its presentation and ask other groups to guess the work setting. After several guesses, have the presenters tell the other groups what their setting is.
  6. Applaud each presentation.

Processing the Activity

- Ask groups what they had to do to demonstrate teamwork in their assigned settings.
- Ask for volunteers to share the kind of teamwork they experience in their own work settings.

Trainer/Facilitator Insights

_____

_____

_____

_____

_____

_____

_____

_____

➤ Section 4

Performing

Performing is the stage of group development during which the real work begins. People are task focused and have a clear idea of the roles they play in the group. When groups reach the Performing stage, they have taken ownership of the group and the work of the group.

During the Norming stage, leaders emerged from the group to guide the work of the team. Often, these are participants who have previous knowledge or skills related to the training material.

Selecting Activities

This is the time of greatest learning for participants, as they have the opportunity to interact with the training material. Some activities in the Performing section encourage participants to share and discuss ideas as they work with new information. Trainers and facilitators will find other activities to help participants learn new material or review old information in a structured way. This section has activities to enhance learning for short training sessions and ongoing teamwork. All activities in the Performing section encourage the active involvement of the participants in their own learning.

The Role of the Trainer/Facilitator

At this point, trainers and facilitators serve more as resources than as directors of the work. However, it is still their responsibility to process the results of the participants' efforts to ensure that there is accurate and complete understanding of the material.

In addition, it is important for the trainer/facilitator to manage time. Assigning times to tasks the participants are involved with and reminding them occasionally of how much time is left is very important. Most training is packed with activities and information. Managing time ensures that all critical information will be covered before the end of the training. Trainers and facilitators are also monitors of the work, to make certain that participants understand the assignment and are on task.

Common Issues in Training and Group Work

What if . . .

- *The activity is not working?* Occasionally, a planned activity is completely outside the range of participants' experiences. Groups become frustrated as they try to understand what is expected of them. When this happens, stop the activity. Say, "This is not working. I would like to try another approach."

- *Groups misunderstand the task and complete it incorrectly?* It is too late to go back. Allow the group to share their work. Tell them that they presented an interesting perspective and then present the correct version of the task.

- *A group is having trouble understanding parts of the training material?* If one group is having problems with a particular section, others may as well. Clarify the material for that group and make a note to review it with all the groups before the end of the training.

- *A group has not completed a task at the end of the time, despite repeated reminders?* You can let them negotiate for a few more minutes. However, don't hold up the whole training until they finish. Instead, suggest that they finish up during break or lunch.

- *There are extreme differences in skill levels among participants?* When this happens, pull the very skilled participants out of their groups and have them serve as coaches for the groups of less skilled participants.

- *You don't have enough training materials for each participant?* This may happen when more than one person is responsible for registration or if walk-ins to the training are allowed. Ask participants to share and, if possible, get more copies run off while the training continues. If copying is not an option, obtain the names and addresses of the participants who did not receive material and arrange to have it mailed after the training.

- *Certification is awarded at the end of the training and people leave early?* Most certification requires the completion of the training. If you will be offering the training again, suggest the participant attend the final part of the next training. Another option is developing an at-home assignment that will allow participants to complete the work independently. However, that option is dependent on the flexibility of the training material.

- *Something unplanned occurs that uses up training time, such as a fire alarm requiring the evacuation of the building?* Revisit the training material and decide what information is most important to cover during the remaining time. Finish up what the group was working on prior to the interruption and then move on with the revised agenda.

Sharing Information

➤ From Personal Experience

Purpose   This activity offers participants the opportunity to share personal experiences related to the subject matter in the training.

Risk Level   Moderate

Time   30 minutes

Number of Participants   Unlimited (small groups of five to seven)

Materials/Preparation   None

Directions
1. Tell participants that most of them have had some personal experience around [subject of the workshop].
2. Ask participants to share that experience within their small groups. For example, if the training has to do with safety, ask participants to share a personal experience they have had related to safety.
3. Ask for volunteers to share their experiences with the larger group.

Processing the Activity
- Ask participants how reflecting on personal experiences with [subject of workshop] will help clarify the learning from the training.
- Ask participants why it is important to make that connection.

Trainer/Facilitator Insights

_____

_____

_____

_____

_____

_____

_____

_____

➤ Hospital Glitch

Purpose   This activity gives participants the opportunity to explore how glitches in procedures are handled.

Risk Level   Moderate

Time   30 minutes

Number of Participants   Thirty maximum (divided as evenly as possible into five groups)

Materials/Preparation

- Index cards with the departments written on them, one per card as follows: Patient Advocacy, Physicians, Pharmacists, Nurses, Couriers

Directions

1. Divide the participants into five groups.
2. Explain that each group will be a department of a large hospital. The hospital has identified a problem with giving patients their prescribed medicine in a timely manner. The normal procedure is for the physicians to prescribe the medicine and give the prescriptions to the nurses. The nurses then send the prescriptions to the pharmacy via courier. The pharmacists fill the prescriptions and send the medications back to the appropriate nurses' stations. The nurses then administer the medications to the patients. Patients often wait more than 24 hours for their medication. The time lapse is especially unacceptable for patients in pain, suffering from infections, or in critical condition. Family members have become involved.
3. Distribute an index card to each group.
4. Tell groups to meet as a "department" to discuss possible sources of this problem and potential solutions. Instruct them to have a note taker to keep an account of their discussion.
5. Ask each group to report to the others.

Processing the Activity

- Ask groups what similarities/differences they noticed in each department's discussion.
- Ask for volunteers to share any similar experiences in the workplace. (The groups meeting as departments are most likely to look at another department as the problem rather than focusing on a solution.)

Trainer/Facilitator Insights

_____

_____

_____

_____

_____

_____

_____

_____

➤ How I Did It

Purpose   This activity allows participants to share problem-solving techniques.

Risk Level   Moderate to High

Time   20 minutes

Number of Participants   Forty maximum

Materials/Preparation
- Flip chart paper and markers for each small group
- Masking tape

Directions
1. Ask participants to share one work problem they have solved with their small groups. They should give no details, but simply state the problem. For example, a group member might say, "I solved the problem of a good secretary who was chronically late for work."
2. Once each group member has shared, ask the groups to choose one of the problems mentioned to hear how it was solved. Hand out flip chart paper and markers and tell groups to list the steps the person took to solve the problem.
3. Use masking tape to post the charted list from each group, and note the differences and similarities in the steps and methods used in problem solving.

Processing the Activity
- Ask participants why it is helpful to hear how others solved problems.
- Ask if anyone wishes to add his or her own steps in problem solving to the posted lists.

Trainer/Facilitator Insights

_____

_____

_____

_____

_____

_____

_____

_____

➤ Idea Swap

Purpose This activity allows participants to move around as they share their good ideas.

Risk Level Low to Moderate

Time 25 minutes

Number of Participants Forty maximum (small groups of six to eight)

Materials/Preparation
- Flip chart paper, two pieces per group
- Assorted markers
- Masking tape
- Paper and pencils for participants

Directions
1. Instruct groups to brainstorm strategies around the topic of the workshop and record them on flip chart paper. For example, if the training has to do with conflict resolution, the brainstorming could be around ways to integrate conflict resolution into the workplace.
2. Give them masking tape to post their brainstormed lists on the walls of the training room.
3. Instruct participants to move around the room with paper and pencils, making notes of good ideas on other groups' brainstorming sheets.
4. When they return to their seats, ask participants if they have questions about the strategies listed on any of the sheets.

Processing the Activity
- Ask for volunteers to share a strategy they noted and how it could work for them back on the job.
- Leave the brainstorming sheets on the wall, telling participants they may revisit them during breaks.

Trainer/Facilitator Insights

_____

_____

_____

_____

_____

_____

_____

_____

➤ I'm Mike

Purpose   This activity is designed to explore the idea that being overly helpful may lead to enabling the recipient of the help to shirk responsibility.

Risk Level   Low

Time   20 minutes

Number of Participants   Unlimited

Materials/Preparation
- A copy of the I'm Mike: The Story handout

Directions
1. Ask for a male volunteer who is willing to stand at the front of the room and read the I'm Mike: The Story handout.
2. Explain that each time a new character is introduced in the story, a volunteer will be asked to join Mike at the front of the room. These characters will not have speaking parts.
3. Tell participants that during the second part of the story, these characters will sit down again.
4. Give the I'm Mike: The Story handout to the volunteer and ask him to begin reading.

Processing the Activity
- Ask participants what Mike's co-workers and family were doing. (They were enabling him to avoid his responsibilities.)
- Ask what kind of problems this kind of "helping" behavior can cause.
- Ask whether anyone has had the experience of helping someone in the workplace shirk his or her responsibilities.

Trainer/Facilitator Insights

_____

_____

_____

_____

_____

_____

_____

_____

I'm Mike: The Story

I'm Mike. I work as sales manager for a manufacturing company. I am married with two little boys. In my spare time I play golf and watch ESPN. It's a great life!

This is my assistant manager. Her name is Sheila. She makes sure that the people in the field meet their quotas. She is on the road working with my salespeople most of the time and is on call 24 hours a day. She is a great assistant.

I'd like you to meet John. John handles all the orders that come in from the sales staff. He regularly works late to make sure orders go out on time. He knows his stuff, so I rarely even check in with him.

This is Tina. She is my administrative assistant. Tina is great at troubleshooting and covers for me all the time. I told her that I have complete faith in her ability to make the right decisions in my absence.

Sam is the vice president of sales and my boss. Great guy! I'm not really good at reports, so he does them for me. He also runs most of the sales meetings.

Meet Lillian. She is my wife and the mother of our two children. Lillian teaches school and still manages to take care of the house and the kids. She even does repairs and painting when it is needed.

Meet Mom. She baby-sits on weekends and in the evening while Lillian runs errands. She also helps Lillian with meals and housework. I couldn't get along without her.

[Pause . . . Motion for everyone else to sit down as you read their names again.]

What a Day!

Mom got a part-time job yesterday. She won't be baby-sitting evenings and weekends anymore. And Lillian has signed up for a Saturday class and tells me I need to be home to watch the boys.

I got in about ten this morning and Sam was waiting in my office. He announced that he was taking on other responsibilities and would no longer write the sales reports nor run tomorrow's sales meeting. I wonder what got into him. I'll have to cancel this afternoon's golf game to get ready for the darn meeting.

On top of everything else, one of our reps called the office before I got in. Tina didn't know how to handle it and referred the rep to Sam. She said Sam asked where I was and she told him she didn't expect me before 10:00 A.M.

I found out John is backlogging orders and we are beginning to get complaints. Seems he was out sick for a while. Someone should have told me.

Well, now I really have a problem. Sheila announced that she has taken a job with another company. Now what will I do?

➤ The Inheritance

Purpose   This activity helps participants practice making decisions as a team.

Risk Level   Low to Moderate

Time   40 minutes

Number of Participants   Forty maximum (divided into six teams)

Materials/Preparation
- Six index cards with descriptions printed on them, one item per card (see Descriptions for Index Cards)

Directions
1. Tell the groups that they will be practicing making decisions as a team.
2. Give each group an index card and ask them to read it over. Tell them that the inheritance came from a favorite teacher that they all had in school.
3. Tell them the rules for the activity are as follows:
   - They are to decide on the best possible use for the property.
   - They can interpret "best use" any way they want. (Note that for some, money may be the decisive factor, but for others it might be environmental, humane, or other considerations.)
   - All members of the team must agree on what to do with their property.
   - They are allowed to make up three additional pieces of information about the property.
   - Team members must be able to state justification for their decisions.
4. Once team members have completed their tasks, ask each group to describe their inheritance, any information they added regarding the property, their joint decision, and justification for the decision.

Processing the Activity
- Ask groups what they had to do to come to a team decision.
- Ask for volunteers to share experiences they have had with team decision making outside of this training.

Trainer/Facilitator Insights

_____

_____

_____

_____

_____

_____

_____

_____

The Inheritance: Descriptions for Index Cards

1. Your team has inherited an uninhabited island in the Caribbean. The island is currently accessible only by boat. Its closest island neighbor is St. Croix in the Virgin Islands, a two-day boat trip away. The island is a nesting ground for sea turtles.

2. Your team has inherited 100 acres of land, including 30 acres of pastureland and a 6-acre lake in a farming community. A large city is 65 miles away. The community is struggling, as many farms have failed in the last decade.

3. Your team has inherited three blocks on the main street of a historic town. The blocks are made up of three-story buildings and storefronts, most of them empty. Some of the buildings have been recognized as having historic significance.

4. Your team has inherited 25 undeveloped acres that include the only mountain in the region. The mountain is an anomaly in an otherwise gently rolling terrain. The land to the east of the mountain drops down to a river and wetlands. North of the mountain, about 45 miles away, is a medium-sized city. Another, smaller city lies 65 miles to the west.

5. Your team has inherited an old restaurant and inn on 5 acres of beachfront property. Zoning laws no longer permit commercial buildings on the beachfront. However, since the inn was in business prior to the zoning laws, it can be used for that purpose, but no other commercial enterprise. The inn has not been open in five years. The beach is experiencing some erosion.

6. Your team has inherited an apartment building in an urban renewal area of a large city. The building has a 90 percent occupancy and nearly 30 percent turnover each month due to transients and eviction for nonpayment of rent. Several families are often living together in one apartment. The building is in need of major repair.

Reviewing Information

In the Middle

Match-Up

Pass It On

Question Ball

Stump 'Em

Three-Ring Circus

Tic Tac Bingo

Tree of Knowledge

What Do You Know?

What's in a Word?

Yesterday and Today

➤ In the Middle

Purpose   This activity allows participants to review at a mid-point in the training.

Risk Level   Low to Moderate

Time   30 minutes

Number of Participants   Forty maximum

Materials/Preparation
- A piece of white poster paper or heavy cardboard, 9 × 12, for each participant
- Markers for each participant

Directions
1. Tell participants to create a place mat with four ideas from this morning, yesterday, or the last two days of training.
2. Once they have completed their place mats, ask them to swap with someone sitting on the other side of the room.
3. Ask for volunteers to read their new place mats aloud.

Processing the Activity
- Ask if anyone received a new place mat with some of his or her own ideas on it. Ask what the ideas were.
- Tell participants to pass their place mats on one more time and to then keep them as a reminder of some of the material they have already covered.

Trainer/Facilitator Insights

_____

_____

_____

_____

_____

_____

_____

_____

➤ Match-Up

Purpose This activity is intended as a review of information presented in the training session.

Risk Level Low to Moderate

Time 20 minutes

Number of Participants Forty maximum

Materials/Preparation
- Index cards
- Identify statements that reflect important points in the training. You should have half as many statements as you have participants. Write half of a statement on one index card and the other half of the statement on a second card. Continue until you have enough cards for half the participants to have the first parts of the statements and half to have the second parts of the statements. For example: *Creating an agenda* (first index card) *helps keep committee members on task* (second index card). Words and definitions or dates and events can be used in place of statement.

Directions
1. Mix up the cards and distribute them, one per participant.
2. Tell participants they need to move around the room and find the person with the index card that will complete their statement.
3. Tell them to help each other with this process.
4. Once participants have paired up to create their statements, ask each pair to read their statement aloud.

Processing the Activity

- Ask participants whether they found the activity difficult or easy and why.
- Ask participants if there is any information from this activity that they would like to review.

Trainer/Facilitator Insights

_____

_____

_____

_____

_____

_____

_____

_____

➤ Pass It On

Purpose   This activity gives participants the opportunity to review vital information from the training session.

Risk Level   Low

Time   10 minutes

Number of Participants   Thirty maximum

Materials/Preparation
- Eight to ten important pieces of information from the training printed on individual index cards

Directions
1. Ask participants to form two lines across the room. There should be an even number of participants in each line. Include yourself if there is an odd number of participants.
2. Explain that you will be handing the first person in each line a card to read silently. Once that person has read the information on the card, he or she should return the card to you.
3. Tell the participants to pass the information down the line by using a low voice to tell the next person the information. When the information reaches the last person in line, he or she should put a hand up.
4. Ask the last person in line to share the information he or she received with the whole group.
5. If the information is not correct, ask the group what the correct version should be.
6. Repeat the process as many times as you wish using the remaining cards.

Processing the Activity

- Ask participants to share any information that was new to them.
- Ask participants if there is information from the training that was not included in the activity that they think is important to remember.

Trainer/Facilitator Insights

_____

_____

_____

_____

_____

_____

_____

_____

➤ Question Ball

Purpose   This activity is an active way for participants to review training information.

Risk Level   High

Time   30 minutes

Number of Participants   Twenty maximum

Materials/Preparation
- Index cards with questions from the training written on them, enough for each participant to have one
- Two wastebaskets
- A timer
- A coin

Space Requirements   Open space

Directions
1. Divide participants into two teams and distribute question cards. Tell them they will be participating in a question-and-answer game and that you will be the referee.
2. Tell teams to move to opposite sides of the room and place a wastebasket in front of each team.
3. Explain that the team that wins the coin toss goes first, and they will be the first team to answer a question posed by a member of the other team. They will have 30 seconds to discuss it. If their answer is correct, they will take the question card from the opposing team and place it in the opposing team's wastebasket, earning a point. If their answer is incorrect, there is no point awarded. Whether the answer is correct or incorrect, the opposing team is up.
4. Tell them you will call time after 10 minutes and the team with the most cards in the opposing team's basket wins.

Note: You will be the person who decides whether an answer is correct or not.

Processing the Activity

- Ask participants if this was a difficult way to review information. Why or why not? (Often, people find it difficult to think under pressure.)
- Ask participants whether they need to go over any of the questions and answers included the game.

Trainer/Facilitator Insights

_____

_____

_____

_____

_____

_____

_____

_____

➤ Stump 'Em

Purpose   This activity gives participants the opportunity to review and interact with the training materials.

Risk Level   Moderate to High

Time   30 minutes

Number of Participants   Thirty-two maximum (divided into four groups)

Materials/Preparation
- Index cards
- Pens or pencils
- Small group prizes

Space Requirements   It important that the groups not be close enough to be able to hear one another, so that the winning teams haven't already heard the correct answers.

Directions
1. Divide participants into four groups and hand out a supply of index cards to each group. Instruct participants to look at the training material and write three questions about the material that they think will stump other groups. They should write the questions on index cards, one per card.
2. Explain that each group will be matched with another group. The group that gets the most answers correct will be the winner of the match.
3. The winners of each match will then challenge each other. The other two teams also play against each other for third and fourth place.
4. The winner of the match between the two first-round winners is the all-round winner.
5. Present prizes to members of the winning group.

Processing the Activity
- Ask participants if they learned anything new.
- Ask participants why it is important to interact with new material.

Trainer/Facilitator Insights

_____

_____

_____

_____

_____

_____

_____

_____

➤ Three-Ring Circus

Purpose   This activity allows participants to present parts of the training material to the whole group.

Risk Level   Low

Time   30 minutes

Number of Participants   Forty maximum (divided into three groups)

Materials/Preparation
- Optional props for groups to use in their presentations

Directions
1. Divide participants into three groups.
2. Explain that they are circus performers. Name each group as clowns, jugglers, or animal trainers.
3. Assign groups different portions of new text (one new "idea") to present in the "circus."
4. Explain that they will present their portion of the material as if they were clowns, jugglers, or animal trainers, depending on the group they are in.
5. Give the teams 10 minutes to prepare; each team has 3 minutes to present.
6. Applaud each effort.

Processing the Activity
- Ask the audience to share what new information they learned from the presentations.
- Ask what areas of the material presented still need clarification.

Trainer/Facilitator Insights

_____

_____

_____

_____

_____

_____

_____

_____

➤ Tic Tac Bingo

Purpose   This activity is a game that involves participants in a review of the material.

Risk Level   Low to Moderate

Time   30 minutes

Number of Participants   Twenty

Materials/Preparation
- A list of questions that correlate with the answers on the boards
- Poster boards (8½ × 11 index stock also works) with answers to questions from training material arranged in a 3 × 3 grid similar to a tic-tac-toe board, one per participant. Boards should have different configurations of the same answers.
- Poker chips or pennies for markers
- Small prizes

Directions
1. Tell participants that they will be playing a version of Bingo.
2. Explain that you will read a question and they will use poker chips or pennies to mark the answer on their boards.
3. Tell them that they can call Bingo when they have a full line across, up/down, or diagonally.
4. Review the answers of the winner and award a prize.

Processing the Activity
- Ask participants whether learning is enhanced by using a game format.
- Ask for any questions that should have been included in the game.

Trainer/Facilitator Insights

_____

_____

_____

_____

_____

_____

_____

_____

➤ Tree of Knowledge

Purpose   This activity helps participants to review important points during the training.

Risk Level   Low

Time   5 minutes per break during the day

Number of Participants   Unlimited

Materials/Preparation
- A picture of a tree with bare branches drawn on large poster board or flip chart paper
- Masking tape
- Leaves cut out of construction paper, four per participant
- Assorted markers
- Tape

   Note: If the group is divided into teams, use different colored leaves for each group.

Directions
1. Hang the poster with masking tape and distribute leaves and markers at the beginning of the training session.
2. Tell participants that before each break they will be asked to identify important information they have gained from the training thus far, write it on a leaf, and tape it to the "tree."
3. Instruct participants to write on their leaves and tape them on the tree before the morning break, before lunch, before the afternoon break, and before the close of training.
4. After each break, review the leaves participants have placed on the tree.

   Note: If the training lasts more than a day, participants can write on their leaves at the close of each day also.

Processing the Activity

- Ask for volunteers to share why they identified particular information as important.
- Ask whether any important information is missing from the tree.

Trainer/Facilitator Insights

_____

_____

_____

_____

_____

_____

_____

_____

➤ What Do You Know?

Purpose   This activity allows participants the opportunity to learn important information from the training session.

Risk Level   Low

Time   15 minutes

Number of Participants   Unlimited

Materials/Preparation
- Index cards or slips of paper with facts from the training written on them, one for each participant. For small groups, make each fact different. For larger groups, duplicate facts if necessary to ensure that everyone has a fact to share.

Directions
1. Give each participant a card with a fact written on it.
2. Explain that when you say "go," participants will move around the room quickly, telling their facts to as many people as possible. For example, in a training about dogs, one participant goes up to another and says, "Did you know that dogs have emotions similar to human emotions?" The other person responds with, "Well, did you know that inbreeding has caused health problems in some breeds?" and so on.
3. At the end of 10 minutes, call time and instruct participants to return to their seats.
4. Ask for volunteers to share something new they learned.

Processing the Activity
- Ask participants why this activity was a good way to learn new information.
- Ask how much of what they learned they think they retained.

Note: Usually visual learners have more difficulty with this activity than auditory learners do.

Trainer/Facilitator Insights

_____

_____

_____

_____

_____

_____

_____

_____

➤ What's in a Word?

Purpose   This activity gives participants an interactive opportunity to review the training material.

Risk Level   Low

Time   20 minutes

Number of Participants   Unlimited (small groups of six to eight)

Materials/Preparation
- Post-it® Notes, three for each participant
- A pen or pencil for each participant

Directions
1. Have participants form small groups. Distribute Post-it Notes and instruct participants to write one letter on each note. Two of the letters should be consonants and one a vowel. There is to be no talking.
2. Instruct small groups to form words with all their letters, Scrabble™-style. They should use as many of their letters as possible.
3. Tell them to relate the words they form to the subject of the training.
4. Ask each group to share their words with the other groups.

Processing the Activity
- Ask participants what they had to do to create relationships between their words and the training material.
- Ask whether anyone gained a new perspective on the training material as a result of this activity.

Trainer/Facilitator Insights

_____

_____

_____

_____

_____

_____

_____

_____

➤ Yesterday and Today

Purpose   This activity gives participants the opportunity to review the previous day's learning. It should be done first thing in the morning of the additional days of training.

Risk Level   Low

Time   25 minutes

Number of Participants   Unlimited

Materials/Preparation
- Flip chart paper
- Assorted markers
- Masking tape

Directions
1. Ask participants to share information they remember from the previous day's training.
2. As participants share, write their responses on flip chart paper.

   Note: You may want to elaborate on their responses, reminding participants of other details related to the information.

3. Title the chart sheets, "Day [number] of [Training Title]."
4. Post the flip chart paper with masking tape and display until the end of the training.

Processing the Activity
- Ask participants why it is important to review material at the beginning of another training day.
- Tell participants that this process will start off the remaining training days.

   Note: If you have assigned homework, this is the time to review it.

Trainer/Facilitator Insights

_____

_____

_____

_____

_____

_____

_____

_____

Learning New Material

À la Mode

Act It Out

An Open Book

The Information Chase

Learning the Language

Napkin Doodles

Personal Time Lines

Scavenger Hunt

Speak the Language

Where Are You Headed?

⊠ À la Mode

Purpose   This activity gives participants the opportunity to work
with the training material to find different ways of presenting it.

Risk Level   Low to Moderate

Time   40 minutes

Number of Participants   Forty maximum (small groups of five to
eight)

Materials/Preparation
- Different types of magazines, one per group
- Paper and a pen or pencil for each group

   Note: Choose magazines with different themes. The following
   themes will work well with this activity: news, sports, women's,
   travel, regional, business, men's, special interest.

Directions
1. Separate participants into small groups. Distribute one magazine
   to each group.
2. Instruct groups to work together to write a mini-article (two or
   three paragraphs) on an important portion of the training
   material to fit the theme of the magazine they received.
3. Invite each group to read its article aloud.
4. Applaud all efforts.

Processing the Activity
- Ask participants what process they used to create the article.
- Ask how well they will remember the training material they had
  to manipulate for the article. Why are they likely to recall the
  information? (Interacting with new material enhances learning.)

Trainer/Facilitator Insights

_____

_____

_____

_____

_____

_____

_____

_____

➤ Act It Out

Purpose   This activity offers participants an opportunity to interact with the material from the training.

Risk Level   Low

Time   60 minutes

Number of Participants   Thirty maximum (divided into five groups)

Materials/Preparation
- Paper and pencils for each group
- Make props available for groups such as hats, paper and markers to make scenery, costume jewelry, or old clothes (optional).

Directions
1. Form five small groups. Assign each group a topic from the training material and hand out paper and pencils.
2. Instruct each group to write a short, one-act play that communicates important information about the topic. Tell them they have 20 minutes.
3. Tell them they will perform their play using all members of their group. Performances should last 3 to 5 minutes each.
4. Once they have completed writing their plays, ask each group to perform.
5. Applaud all efforts.

Processing the Activity
- Ask participants whether or not they learned anything new about their topic when working on their plays.
- Ask why it is important to interact with new material. (Interacting with new material reinforces new learning.)

Trainer/Facilitator Insights

_____

_____

_____

_____

_____

_____

_____

_____

➤ An Open Book

Purpose   This activity directs participants to do research with the training material.

Risk Level   Moderate

Time   30 minutes or more

Number of Participants   Forty maximum

Materials/Preparation
- Questions chosen from the material written on separate pieces of flip chart paper. The number of questions posted will determine the length of time needed for this activity. Questions should require that participants research the training material.
- Masking tape
- Different colored pads of Post-it® Notes, one color for each small group
- Pens for each group

Directions
1. Post the pieces of flip chart paper in different areas of the room using masking tape. Distribute a different colored Post-it Note pad to each group.
2. Explain that the answers to the questions posted on the chart paper can be found in the training material.
3. Instruct groups to research each question, write the answer on one of their Post-it Notes, and stick the note under the question listed on chart paper. Emphasize that all group members must participate in researching each question so that the entire group will know the answer to each question.
4. Tell participants how much time they will have to work, based on the number of questions you decide to post.
5. Review each question and the answers that the groups have given.

Processing the Activity

- Ask for volunteers to share what new information they learned.
- Ask groups to share how they managed their work.

Trainer/Facilitator Insights

_____

_____

_____

_____

_____

_____

_____

_____

➤ The Information Chase

Purpose   This activity should be done early in the training session, as it allows participants to interact with new material or a new manual in order to become familiar with the contents.

Risk Level   Low

Time   45 minutes

Number of Participants   Unlimited (small groups of six to eight)

Materials/Preparation
- Copies of the Information Chase Worksheet, one per participant
- A pen or pencil for each participant

Note: Pull information from the training material/manual and insert in appropriate places on the worksheet. Be sure to pull from the entire manual or all material used in the training session. If desired, you may change the number and type of questions to better fit the training material/manual.

Directions
1. Tell participants that they will be working with the material to find the information requested on the worksheets. If you have extensive material to cover, assign a section of the worksheet to each small group.
2. Tell participants they have 30 minutes and to begin.
3. Ask each group to report on its findings.

Processing the Activity
- Ask participants how this activity was helpful to their understanding of the manual/material. (It exposed participants to the whole of material/manual, including information the training may not cover.)

- Ask participants anything they noticed about the format of the material.
- Ask what questions they still have about the material.

Trainer/Facilitator Insights

_____

_____

_____

_____

_____

_____

_____

_____

Information Chase Worksheet

1. How many chapters or sections are included in this material?

2. What is the title of chapter/section _____? What is one important point in this chapter/section?

3. What is the title of chapter/section _____? What is one important point in this chapter/section?

4. Explain the following three words/phrases. Note the pages on which they are found.

   _____

   _____

   _____

5. Find the chapter/section on _____ and note what it is about and pages on which it is found.

6. Give a brief explanation of chapter/section _____ .

7. What is the last chapter/section in the manual/material? Why is it the last chapter/section?

8. Where in the material do you find _____? Note page numbers.

9. What are the key points in chapter _____?

10. Do you have a question about the material you looked over in the manual? Write it below.

➤ Learning the Language

Purpose   This activity is designed to help participants become familiar with terms that will be used in the training session.

Risk Level   Low

Time   10 minutes

Number of Participants   Unlimited

Materials/Preparation
- On plain paper (8½ × 11), list ten words that are related to the subject of the training. Between the words, leave space in which participants can write. Make enough copies for each participant to have one.
- Write the definitions for the words on individual pieces of flip chart paper and post around the room.
- Provide paper and pencils for each participant.

  Note: This activity can be made more challenging by posting more definitions than there are words on the list.

Directions
1. As participants arrive, give each a word list.
2. Explain that there are definitions for the words posted around the room.
3. Tell participants to find the definitions that match the words on their lists and write them down.
4. Tell them to do this activity before the training starts.

Processing the Activity
- Welcome participants to the training.
- Explain that the words on the handouts they received when they arrived are part of the vocabulary of the training.
- Tell them that they will have the opportunity to check their answers as the training progresses.

- At the end of the training, ask participants whether they all have correct definitions for the words on their lists.

Trainer/Facilitator Insights

_____

_____

_____

_____

_____

_____

_____

_____

➤ Napkin Doodles

Purpose   This activity offers participants a fun way of interacting
with the information offered in the training.

Risk Level   Low

Time   25 minutes

Number of Participants   Unlimited (small groups of six to eight)

Materials/Preparation
- Plain white cocktail napkins (a few for each small group)
- Colored pens or markers

Directions
1. Form groups and hand out the napkins and pens. Explain to participants that some napkins come imprinted with clever slogans and sayings. (Hold up an example if you have one.)
2. Instruct each small group to do its own napkin design or slogan based on the information gained in the training, for example: "If I can't meet my quota in heaven, I'm not going."

Processing the Activity
- Ask each group to share its slogan or design with the rest of the participants.
- Ask groups why they chose the information they did for their napkins.

Trainer/Facilitator Insights

_____

_____

_____

_____

_____

_____

_____

_____

⊒ Personal Time Lines

Purpose   This activity is a good introduction to the material to be
   presented in a workshop.

Risk Level   Low to Moderate

Time   30 minutes

Number of Participants   Unlimited (small groups of six to eight)

Materials/Preparation
   • Plain paper for each participant
   • A pen or pencil for each participant

Directions
   1. Explain to participants that most people know something about
      [subject of the workshop].
   2. Instruct the participants to draw a line across their pieces of
      paper. Tell them that this is their personal time line, beginning
      in high school and ending today. They may want to mark their
      time lines by using dates or events such as high school, college,
      first job, and so forth.
   3. Ask participants to mark the point at which they first learned
      something about [subject of the workshop]. Tell them to add
      more marks along their time line where they may have gained
      additional information.
   4. Instruct participants to briefly share in their groups what they
      know to this point about [subject of the workshop].

Processing the Activity
   • Ask participants why it is important to reflect on previous
     knowledge.
   • Ask whether anyone had no prior knowledge of the workshop
     material.
   • Ask whether anyone was extremely well versed in [subject of the
     workshop].

Trainer/Facilitator Insights

_____

_____

_____

_____

_____

_____

_____

_____

⊒ Scavenger Hunt

Purpose This activity gives participants an active and entertaining way to review or gain new information.

Risk Level Moderate to High

Time 20 minutes

Number of Participants Twenty to thirty

Materials/Preparation
- Sets of four index cards with different, connected information related to the training material on each card. For example: Four cards related to doing needs assessment could be "gathering data, organizing data, identifying strengths, identifying deficiencies." The number of sets of cards is dictated by the number of participants, as you'll need one set per participant.
- Use the same information on every two sets of cards.

Directions
1. Before the training day begins, hide the index cards around the training room or area near the training room. Cards should be hidden in separate places unless they are from different sets of information.
2. Tell participants that they will be going on a scavenger hunt.
3. Explain that index cards are hidden around the training area. Each card has one piece of a set of information.
4. Each participant is to find a set of four cards with related information. Tell participants they have 8 minutes to find a complete set of cards.
5. At the end of 8 minutes, call time.
6. Ask for volunteers to read the information cards they found.

Processing the Activity
- Ask participants whether they learned anything new from the information cards.
- Ask for volunteers to share how this hunt differed from others in which they have participated.

Trainer/Facilitator Insights

_____

_____

_____

_____

_____

_____

_____

_____

➤ Speak the Language

Purpose   This activity has small groups of participants teaching other groups portions of the training material.

Risk Level   Moderate

Time   45 to 60 minutes

Number of Participants   Forty maximum (small groups of six to eight)

Materials/Preparation
- Selected text from training materials, one section per small group

Directions
1. Choose and assign different parts of the training material to each small group.
2. Explain that they will be teaching their sections to the larger group.
3. Tell them they should prepare their lessons as if the audience has a limited understanding of English. No slang or office lingo, jargon, or acronyms should be used.
4. Allow groups 20 to 25 minutes to prepare.
5. Ask each group to present its portion of the material.
6. Applaud all efforts.

Processing the Activity
- Ask participants how well they understand the portion of the text they presented.
- Ask participants how well they understand the information presented to them.
- Ask what happens when we use our workplace lingo outside of the workplace.

Trainer/Facilitator Insights

_____

_____

_____

_____

_____

_____

_____

_____

➤ Where Are You Headed?

Purpose This activity encourages participants to plan how they will use the training material in their workplaces.

Risk Level Moderate

Time 25 minutes

Number of Participants Unlimited

Materials/Preparation
- 9 × 12 pieces of lightweight cardboard or paper, one per participant
- A pencil or marker for each participant

Directions
1. Give everyone a piece of paper and a pencil or marker. Tell participants to turn the paper so that the 12-inch side is horizontal and have them draw a straight line from one end to the other.
2. Explain that the left end of the line is the training they are participating in now. They are learning new information or skills now that they will take back to their workplaces.
3. Ask them to write the word "training" at the left end of their line.
4. At the right end of the line, tell them to write the word "accomplishment."
5. Now ask them to look at what steps they will have to take to implement the new learning.
6. Ask them to record the steps as they would on a time line.
7. Once they have written the steps they will take to implement the new learning, ask them to write what they will have accomplished in place of the word "accomplishment."
8. Invite volunteers to share their plans with the whole group.

Processing the Activity

- Ask participants how many use this kind of planning process in their personal lives.
- Ask why some people find this kind of planning helpful both personally and professionally.

Trainer/Facilitator Insights

_____

_____

_____

_____

_____

_____

_____

_____

⊒ Section 5

Adjourning

The Need for Closure

The process of group development described in the last four sections builds relationships among group members. Participants have bonded and, at the end of the training or group work, will need to say goodbye to one another. The Adjourning section offers structured activities for ending training sessions and group work. These activities serve as a bridge back to the workplace or home. Some of them encourage participants to explore how they will use the new learning after they leave the training. Other activities help participants keep the connections they made with others during the training. Adjourning activities are a structured way to ensure the greatest use of the new skills and information later on. Without some kind closure, the training becomes an experience that is separate and apart from the participants' everyday lives.

Selecting Activities

The longer the group has been together, the stronger are their relationships with one another. They have a sense of themselves as an entity and have formed remarkably strong bonds. These groups need the time as well as the opportunity to say goodbye. In these long-term groups, there are often strong needs to affirm relationships that have formed and express appreciation for the support of the group. There may be some participants for whom the experience of relating to others is profound. These people are usually reserved or shy. Closure eases them away from the group while still affirming their participation and the relationships they formed.

The adjourning activities range from brief to involved, depending on the needs of the group. Shorter adjourning activities include quick, upbeat endings and briefly expressed farewells. These are appropriate for groups that have been together for just a few hours. Other "Saying Goodbye" activities are celebrations or opportunities to express feelings about the experience or about fellow participants. These activities are suited for groups or teams that have been together for longer periods of time. There is also a section on "Keeping in Touch," which gives participants opportunities to exchange contact information or make plans to reconnect in the weeks to come.

"Self-Reflection" activities encourage participants to look at accomplishments and new learning that occurred during their time in the group. These activities are a form of self-assessment. Activities to assess the training are also offered. In addition, however, trainers and facilitators should provide forms that allow participants to give a comprehensive evaluation of their experience with the training or team.

An effective way to help participants bridge the gap between the training or group and the workplace is to allow time for planning as part of the closure. Activities found in the "Applying Learning" section provide structured ways for participants to look ahead.

Making Time for Closure

There is no training or group meeting, no matter how brief, that does not require some form of closure. It might be simply a summary of what was accomplished or a word from each participant. People need the experience of ending the task or commitment so they can move on to the next thing.

Responses to the concept of closure by trainers and participants vary greatly. Trainers may see these activities as too time-consuming, while participants may just be resistant to ending the experience. Build a closure activity into the agenda. If the activity has its own time slot, it is less likely to be omitted. Also, assuring participants that they have the freedom to continue their relationships outside of the training and encouraging them to exchange e-mail addresses and phone numbers will reduce resistance to saying goodbye.

Common Issues in Training and Group Work

What if . . .

- *People leave early and will not be participating in the group closure?* Include these participants in the closing activity in absentia. These people are still connected to group members who need an opportunity to express their feelings about the missing participants. Group members can also be encouraged to write something to the missing members to be sent to them after the training is over.

- *Some participants are very critical of the training they received?* Thank them for the feedback and encourage them to put it in writing. It is important to hear the negative as well as the positive feedback in order to correct or improve the content or style of the training.

- *Participants linger after the training beyond a reasonable time?* Ask that the group move their conversation to another area.

Saying Goodbye

Bus Boys and Girls

Cheers

Collectible Items II

Fast Finish

Fortune Telling

Gift Giving

Memories

Off into the Sunset

Parting Is Such Sweet Sorrow

A Penny for Your Thoughts

Present the Awards

Self-Portrait Continued

A Toast

➤ Bus Boys and Girls

Purpose   This activity gives participants a chance to move around while cleaning up the room.

Risk Level   Low

Time   5 minutes

Number of Participants   Unlimited (divided by table groups of six to eight)

Materials/Preparation
- Wastebasket
- Candy or other prizes for a team

Directions
1. Tell participants that when you say "go" they will bus their tables and clean up the floor around the tables. They should bring all extra handouts, markers, and other supplies to the front of the room. Take-home materials should be organized and ready to go.
2. Explain that the first team to complete their cleanup "wins."
3. Say "go."
4. Give the prizes to the winning team.

Processing the Activity
- Tell the teams that this activity was just one more example of the good teamwork they have demonstrated during the training.
- Continue with evaluation or other closing activities.
- Thank everyone and say goodbye.

Trainer/Facilitator Insights

_____

_____

_____

_____

_____

_____

_____

_____

➤ Cheers

Purpose This activity gives participants one last opportunity to work together and offers an enjoyable way to close the training.

Risk Level Low

Time 30 minutes

Number of Participants Forty (small groups of six to eight)

Materials/Preparation None

Directions

1. Instruct each group to devise a short cheer to celebrate the completion of the training; for example: "We worked hard and we learned great stuff; now its time to go 'cause enough is enough!"
2. Give each group an opportunity to perform and applaud all efforts.

Processing the Activity

- Tell participants that they brought the same energy and creativity to the cheers that they have demonstrated throughout the training.
- Thank them for their good work and say goodbye.

Trainer/Facilitator Insights

_____

_____

_____

_____

_____

_____

_____

➤ Collectible Items II

Purpose   This activity is the completion of the Collectible Items activity from the Forming section. It helps bring closure to the training day by having groups share their collections with others.

Risk Level   Low to Moderate

Time   15 minutes

Number of Participants   Thirty (small groups of four to six)

Materials/Preparation
- Bags of items collected during training

Directions
1. Tell participants to share the contents of their bags with group members.
2. Instruct them to share anything they remember about the people who gave them the items.
3. Say that it is time to say goodbye to their group.
4. Once they have completed their group goodbyes, tell them to say goodbye to some of the people they spoke with during their collecting. Give them 5 minutes to speak to as many people as possible.

Processing the Activity
- Ask participants what was valuable about this activity. (One response should be getting to meet people outside of their small groups.)
- Thank participants for their involvement in the training and say goodbye.

Trainer/Facilitator Insights

_____

_____

_____

_____

_____

_____

_____

_____

➤ Fast Finish

Purpose   This activity is a quick form of closure good for short
training sessions.

Risk Level   Low

Time   10 minutes

Number of Participants   Forty maximum

Materials/Preparation   None

Directions
1. Ask participants to stand.
2. Ask each person to say his or her name and one thing he or she
   learned during the training.

Processing the Activity
- With everyone standing, thank participants and wave goodbye.

Trainer/Facilitator Insights

_____

_____

_____

_____

_____

_____

_____

_____

➤ Fortune Telling

Purpose   This activity gives participants the opportunity to receive positive feedback about themselves.

Risk Level   Moderate

Time   15 minutes

Number of Participants   Unlimited

Materials/Preparation   None

Directions
1. Explain to participants that it is time to say goodbye.
2. Tell participants to choose partners from within their working groups.
3. Ask participants to think of one positive quality about their partner and what that quality could mean to his or her future. Use an example: "During this workshop, you have demonstrated great writing skills. I see a best-selling novel in your future."
4. Tell the participants to tell their partners about their positive qualities.

Processing the Activity
- Ask whether anyone heard something about himself or herself that was surprising.
- Ask for volunteers to share how they felt about what their partners said to them.
- Thank everyone and say goodbye.

Trainer/Facilitator Insights

_____

_____

_____

_____

_____

_____

_____

_____

➤ Gift Giving

Purpose   This activity gives participants the opportunity to write personal messages to other group members at the close of the training.

Risk Level   High

Time   30 minutes

Number of Participants   Thirty maximum (divided into five groups)

Materials/Preparation
- One business-sized envelope for each participant
- A pen or pencil for each participant
- Plain paper cut in strips (thirty-six to forty-two strips per team) or ten or more small note pads

Directions
1. Distribute envelopes and ask participants to write their names on them.
2. Distribute paper strips or note pads.
3. Tell participants that they should write positive, personal messages to each person in their group and place the messages in that person's envelope.
4. Once all participants have completed the message writing at their tables, invite them to write messages for other participants they have come to know.

Processing the Activity
- Ask participants whether anyone has a verbal message for the whole group.
- Give your own verbal message to the group.
- Tell participants to take their envelopes with them when they leave and enjoy the positive messages they have received.

Trainer/Facilitator Insights

_____

_____

_____

_____

_____

_____

_____

_____

➤ Memories

Purpose　This activity encourages participants and trainer to give positive feedback to one another.

Risk Level　Moderate

Time　10 to 15 minutes

Number of Participants　Thirty maximum

Materials/Preparation　None

Directions
1. Tell participants that there were lots of memorable moments during the training.
2. Ask them to think about the three most memorable moments for them during the training.
3. Tell them your own three high points for the training.
4. Ask each participant to share with the entire group.

Processing the Activity
• Thank participants for sharing and say goodbye.

Trainer/Facilitator Insights

_____

_____

_____

_____

_____

_____

_____

_____

⊒ Off into the Sunset

Purpose   This activity offers a pleasant, peaceful way to end a
training session.

Risk Level   Low

Time   10 minutes

Number of Participants   Unlimited

Materials/Preparation
- A soothing tape or CD, perhaps the sounds of waves crashing on
  the beach
- A tape or CD player
- An evaluation form for each participant
- A pen or pencil for each participant

Directions
1. Thank participants for their work in the training.
2. Explain that you will be turning the lights down a little bit and
   playing a tape as they fill out their evaluations.
3. Tell them that if they talk to one another, they should keep
   their voices low.
4. Explain that you hope this closure will help them make a
   comfortable transition from the training back to work and
   home.
5. Distribute the evaluation forms and pens or pencils.
6. Lower the lights and begin the tape or CD.
7. At the end of 10 minutes, turn the lights back up and the
   tape off.
8. Collect the evaluation forms.

Processing the Activity
- Say goodbye.

Trainer/Facilitator Insights

_____

_____

_____

_____

_____

_____

_____

_____

➤ Parting Is Such Sweet Sorrow

Purpose   This activity gives participants the opportunity for celebration at the end of a 3-, 4-, or 5-day training program.

Risk Level   Low

Time   20 minutes

Number of Participants   Unlimited

Materials/Preparation
   • Request that people bring something sweet or savory to the last day of training. Assign a few participants to bring paper plates, cups, napkins, and drinks. Set up a table to serve as the buffet.

Directions
   1. Tell participants that they have worked hard for the last few days and it is time to celebrate.
   2. Invite them to take this time for celebrating with other participants.
   3. Once participants are served, lead them in toasts to their accomplishments.

Processing the Activity
   • Thank participants for their hard work and say goodbye.

Trainer/Facilitator Insights

_____

_____

_____

_____

_____

_____

_____

➤ A Penny for Your Thoughts

Purpose   This activity allows participants to say goodbye to others in their own ways.

Risk Level   High

Time   10 minutes

Number of Participants   Twenty-five maximum

Materials/Preparation
- Pennies, enough for one for each participant and for the trainer

Directions
1. Tell participants that it is time to say goodbye.
2. Tell them you will give them a penny for their thoughts about their experiences during the training or with other participants.
3. Give participants pennies as they share.
4. Save a penny for yourself and share your thoughts with participants.

Processing the Activity
- Tell participants to take these positive comments with them when they leave.
- Thank participants for sharing and say goodbye.

Trainer/Facilitator Insights

_____

_____

_____

_____

_____

_____

_____

➤ Present the Awards

Purpose　This activity is an upbeat way for a small group to end a training session.

Risk Level　Low to Moderate

Time　10 minutes

Number of Participants　Fifteen maximum

Materials/Preparation
- Certificates, one per participant, in the following categories: Most congenial, most creative, neatest, best dressed, funniest, best smile, best contributor (could be most talkative), best idea, wisest, healthiest, most artistic, most wonderful, greatest, most charming, most talented (add to or change the adjectives, if desired)

Directions
1. Present the appropriate certificate to each participant.
2. Applaud each recipient.

Processing the Activity
- Tell participants they were all great, charming, talented, and wonderful. Thank them and say goodbye.

Trainer/Facilitator Insights

_____

_____

_____

_____

_____

_____

_____

➤ Self-Portrait Continued

Purpose   This activity should be used in conjunction with the activity entitled Self-Portrait found in the Forming section. It reminds participants of the people they met during the training session or during group work.

Risk Level   Low to Moderate

Time   10 minutes

Number of Participants   Unlimited (small groups of six to eight)

Materials/Preparation
- See activity entitled Self-Portrait in the Forming section.

Directions
1. Tell participants to revisit others' self-portraits on the wall and write a few final words. They may want to include their names and a means of contact.
2. Once participants have completed writing their messages to others, they should remove their own portraits from the wall to take home.

Processing the Activity
- Tell participants that these self-portraits will serve as wonderful reminders of the people they met during the training.
- Congratulate the whole group on a job well done and say goodbye.

Trainer/Facilitator Insights

_____

_____

_____

_____

_____

_____

_____

_____

➤ A Toast

Purpose   This activity is a quick closure to a short training session.

Risk Level   Low

Time   5 minutes

Number of Participants   Unlimited

Materials/Preparation
- A copy of A Toast: Drink a Toast for the facilitator

Directions
1. Tell participants that it is time to say goodbye and that you would like to make a toast to the work they have done together.
2. Read the poem.

   Note: In lieu of reading the prepared toast, you could invite participants to make their own toasts as a closure to the training.

Processing the Activity
- Ask whether anyone else would like to make a toast.
- Thank everyone and say goodbye.

Trainer/Facilitator Insights

_____

_____

_____

_____

_____

_____

_____

A Toast: Drink a Toast

Let's raise our glasses to drink a toast,

First acknowledging our host.

Now let's recognize our friends

And thank them as this training ends.

Safe journeys 'til we meet again.

Self-Reflection

Dear Diary: Closure

Growing Up

Lost and Found

Pack Your Bags

Tuck Away II

You Deserve a Medal

➤ Dear Diary: Closure

Purpose This activity is a follow-up to the Dear Diary: Getting Started activity found in the Forming section. It is designed to help participants reflect on the learning gained and experiences they had during the training. Trainers should use this activity for training lasting longer than one day.

Risk Level Moderate

Time 30 minutes

Number of Participants Twenty-five maximum

Materials/Preparation
- Participants should have written reflections from each day of training.

Directions
1. Tell participants that the training is coming to an end.
2. Ask them to look at the journals they kept during the training and identify new learning or experiences they want to share with the group.
3. Make sure everyone has the opportunity to share.

Processing the Activity
- Note the variety of information shared by participants.
- Ask whether anyone would like to say something personal to the rest of the group.
- Say your own goodbye to the group.

Trainer/Facilitator Insights

_____

_____

_____

_____

_____

_____

_____

_____

⊐ Growing Up

Purpose   This activity encourages participants to look at their own growth as a result of the training.

Risk Level   Moderate to High

Time   15 minutes

Number of Participants   Forty maximum

Materials/Preparation
- Paper for each participant
- A pencil or marker for each participant

Directions
1. Tell participants that you hope they have experienced growth as a result of the training.
2. Hand out paper and pencils, and ask them to chart that growth from infancy (when they walked in the door) through childhood and adolescence (learning during training) to adulthood (the end of the training).
3. Ask them to think about what they knew when they came in, what they learned over the course of the training, and where they are now.
4. Ask for volunteers to share their charts.

Processing the Activity
- Ask whether anyone experienced more growth than he or she expected as a result of the training.
- Thank participants and say goodbye.

Trainer/Facilitator Insights

_____

_____

_____

_____

_____

_____

_____

_____

➤ Lost and Found

Purpose   This activity asks participants to evaluate what has changed for them as a result of the training.

Risk Level   High

Time   20 minutes

Number of Participants   Unlimited (small groups of six to eight)

Materials/Preparation   None

Directions
1. Tell participants that every learning experience changes us in some way.
2. Instruct them to share in their small groups things they may have let go of as a result of this training and things they learned—what they have lost and what they have found.
3. Give them an example: "As a result of this training, I have learned that teamwork is a great way for accomplishing a multitude of tasks and given up the idea that I have to do everything myself."
4. Ask each group to share what their group members had to say.

Processing the Activity
- Ask participants why new learning sometimes means giving up (or losing) something as well as learning something new.
- Thank everyone for participating and say goodbye.

Trainer/Facilitator Insights

_____

_____

_____

_____

_____

_____

_____

_____

➤ Pack Your Bags

Purpose   This activity gives participants the opportunity to share what they will take away from the training.

Risk Level   Low to Moderate

Time   20 minutes

Number of Participants   Unlimited (small groups of six to eight)

Materials/Preparation
- Plain white paper or copies of the Pack Your Bags handout, one per participant
- A pen or pencil for each participant

Directions
1. Tell participants to think about what they will take away from this training.
2. Ask them to write the list of things they will take away on a piece of plain paper or the handout.
3. Instruct participants to share what they packed in their bags with their small groups.
4. Ask for volunteers to share with the larger group.

Processing the Activity
- Tell participants that sometimes the most valuable thing we pack in our bags at the end of a training experience is the connections we made with others.
- Thank everyone for a job well done and say goodbye.

Trainer/Facilitator Insights

_____

_____

_____

_____

_____

_____

_____

Pack Your Bags

➤ Tuck Away II

Purpose   This activity is a follow-up to Tuck Away in the Forming section. It helps participants problem-solve concerns they brought with them at the start of the training or group.

Risk Level   Low to Moderate

Time   10 minutes

Number of Participants   Unlimited

Materials/Preparation
- Envelopes with participants' names on them from the Tuck Away activity found in the Forming section

Directions
1. Distribute the envelopes to participants.
2. Ask them to look at the concerns, worries, and responsibilities they wrote about at the beginning of the training.
3. Ask them if they have a different perspective on anything they wrote and whether they want to add or subtract from their lists.
4. Instruct participants to choose one of the problems they wrote about and spend a few minutes problem solving.
5. Ask for volunteers to share a problem and a solution with the rest of the group.

Processing the Activity
- Tell participants that sometimes getting their minds off troubling issues for a while gives them a clearer perspective when they revisit those issues.
- Say that you hope they are all energized by their experience with the training.

Trainer/Facilitator Insights

_____

_____

_____

_____

_____

_____

_____

_____

➤ You Deserve a Medal

Purpose   This activity gives participants the opportunity to summarize accomplishments and new learning gained from the training.

Risk Level   Low

Time   30 minutes

Number of Participants   Twenty-five maximum (small groups of five)

Materials/Preparation
- A plain stick-on name tag or an index card for each participant
- Tape
- Colored markers

Directions
1. Distribute blank name tags or index cards and tape, as well as colored markers.
2. Explain that participants deserve medals for their participation in the training.
3. Tell them to make themselves medals using the distributed materials. They should include a few words or symbols on their medals that reflect things they accomplished or new learning they gained during the training.
4. Allow 10 minutes for participants to complete their medals.
5. Ask participants to share their medals in their small groups.

   Note: The whole group can share if you have only ten or twelve participants.

Processing the Activity
- If participants are grouped, ask for volunteers from each group to share some commonalities and differences in new learning and accomplishments.

- Instruct participants to wear their medals as a reminder of the work they did.
- Thank participants and say goodbye.

Trainer/Facilitator Insights

_____

_____

_____

_____

_____

_____

_____

_____

_____

Assessing Training

Headlines

High Points

Letter Writing Continued

➤ Headlines

Purpose   This activity helps participants think about the key learning that occurred during the training.

Risk Level   Low

Time   20 minutes

Number of Participants   Unlimited (small groups of six to eight)

Materials/Preparation
- Plain paper for each participant
- A marker for each participant

Directions
1. Distribute paper and markers.
2. Tell participants that it is important to review key learning as the training session comes to a close.
3. Ask them to think of each piece of paper as the front page of a newspaper.
4. Explain that the most important news of the day is headlined on the front page and you want them to design a front page with headlines reflecting the most important information from the training.
5. Once they have completed their front pages, ask them to share them with their groups.

Processing the Activity
- Ask for volunteers to share their front pages with the whole group.
- Ask how participants decided what was front-page information.
- Compliment participants on their hard work and say goodbye.

Trainer/Facilitator Insights

_____

_____

_____

_____

_____

_____

_____

_____

➤ High Points

Purpose   This activity is designed as a review and evaluation of the training.

Risk Level   Low

Time   15 minutes

Number of Participants   Unlimited (small groups of four to six)

Materials/Preparation
- One copy of the High Points Handout for each participant
- A pen or pencil for each participant

Directions
1. Distribute High Points handouts and ask participants to fill them out.
2. Once they have finished, tell participants to share one high point with members of their small group.

Processing the Activity
- If this has been a multi-day training session, ask for one person from each group to share a high point of the first day.
- Ask for a different person from each group to share a high point of the small group.
- Ask for another person from each group to share a high point of the material.
- Ask another person from each group to share a high point of the training.
- Share your own high points from the training and say goodbye.

Trainer/Facilitator Insights

_____

_____

_____

_____

_____

_____

_____

High Points Handout

(If appropriate) A high point of the first day of training was . . .

A high point of my small group was . . .

A high point of the material provided was . . .

A high point of the training was . . .

➤ Letter Writing Continued

Purpose   This activity is a follow-up to the Letter Writing activity in the Forming section. It allows participants to write letters back to the trainer, sharing what they liked and what could be improved.

Risk Level   Moderate

Time   10 minutes

Number of Participants   Unlimited

Materials/Preparation
- Plain paper, one piece for each participant
- A pen or pencil for each participant

Directions
1. Ask participants if they remember receiving a letter from you at the start of the training session.
2. Tell them that you now want them to write back to you, telling you what they liked or would change about the training. Hand out paper and pens or pencils and give everyone 5 minutes to write their thoughts.
3. Ask for volunteers to share parts of their letters.

Processing the Activity
- Collect the letters to use for improvement in the content or design of future training.
- Thank participants and say goodbye.

Trainer/Facilitator Insights

_____

_____

_____

_____

_____

_____

_____

_____

Applying Learning

⊠ Coming Attractions

Purpose   This activity gives participants the opportunity to plan what they will do with their new skills/information.

Risk Level   Low to Moderate

Time   20 minutes

Number of Participants   Thirty maximum (small groups of five or six)

Materials/Preparation   None

Directions
1. Tell participants to think about how they will use the new skills/information they learned in the training when they are back home.
2. Ask them to put their plans in the form of coming attractions; for example: "Coming soon to an office near you, new and better software. Debuting on February 21, at 10:00 A.M. in the computer lab. Don't miss it!"
3. When they have completed their coming attractions, ask participants to share in their small group.
4. Ask each small group to share one coming attraction with the larger group.

Processing the Activity
- Wish participants luck with their coming attractions.
- Thank everyone and say goodbye.

Trainer/Facilitator Insights

_____

_____

_____

_____

_____

_____

_____

_____

➤ A Contract with Myself

Purpose   This activity is designed to start participants thinking about how they will use the information/skills they learned during the training.

Risk Level   Low to Moderate

Time   25 minutes

Number of Participants   Unlimited (small groups of six to eight)

Materials/Preparation
- One copy of the Contract with Myself Handout for each participant
- A pen or pencil for each participant

Directions
1. Distribute one Contract with Myself handout and a pen or pencil to each participant. Ask participants to complete the statements on the handouts.
2. Instruct participants to share their completed statements in their small groups.

Processing the Activity
- Ask for volunteers to share any ideas they heard that were especially inspiring.
- Wish participants success with their plans and say goodbye.

Trainer/Facilitator Insights

_____

_____

_____

_____

_____

_____

Contract with Myself Handout

Name:

1. Immediately after this workshop, I plan to use the information/skills I learned here to . . .

2. In the next year, I plan to be using the new information/skills I learned to . . .

3. Five years from now, I will be using the information/skills I learned in this workshop to . . .

Signed:

➤ Map of Success

Purpose   This activity directs participants to review what they have learned and how they will use it in the workplace.

Risk Level   Moderate

Time   30 minutes

Number of Participants   Unlimited

Materials/Preparation
- Flip chart paper and a marker
- One piece of legal-size paper for each participant
- A marker for each participant

Directions
1. Tell participants that they have come to the end of a journey.
2. Explain that you would like them to draw maps of the journey and include where they will be going from here.
3. Demonstrate by drawing a map on flip chart paper. Say that the left side of the paper represents the start of the training. Draw a short wavy horizontal line (about an inch) on the left side of the paper, and write the first important information covered in the training. Continue across the paper toward the right, adding information learned in the training. At the right side of the paper write "workplace." At that point write what participants might do with the information when they go back to their workplaces. Note that each person's important information will be different. Participants may add other bits of information or symbols to their own maps.
4. Give them 10 minutes to draw their maps.
5. Ask participants to share their maps with the person sitting next to them.

Processing the Activity

- Ask for volunteers to share what they will be doing with the information at their workplaces.
- Wish them luck and say goodbye.

Trainer/Facilitator Insights

_____

_____

_____

_____

_____

_____

_____

_____

➤ Walls and Windows

Purpose   This activity encourages participants to identify opportunities as well as obstacles to putting their new learning into practice.

Risk Level   Low to Moderate

Time   20 minutes

Number of Participants   Unlimited (small groups of five or six)

Materials/Preparation   None

Directions
1. Ask participants to think about the opportunities (windows) and the obstacles (walls) they may have to using what they have learned back home.
2. Ask them to share within their small groups for about 10 minutes.
3. Ask for volunteers to share their "walls and windows" with the larger group.

Processing the Activity
- Thank the group for their participation and wish them many more windows than walls.
- Say goodbye.

Trainer/Facilitator Insights

_____

_____

_____

_____

_____

_____

_____

Keeping in Touch

In the Circle

Make a Date

➤ In the Circle

Purpose   This activity allows participants to arrange for post-training contacts with other participants.

Risk Level   Moderate

Time   10 minutes

Number of Participants   Thirty maximum

Materials/Preparation
- Index cards, one per participant
- A pen or pencil for each participant

Directions
1. Distribute index cards and instruct participants to write their names, phone numbers, and/or e-mail addresses on the index cards.
2. Ask participants to stand and make a circle.
3. Tell them that they will pass their index cards to the left when they hear "go" and stop passing when they hear "stop."
4. Call "stop" when cards are about halfway around the circle.
5. Explain that the cards participants end up with identify their contacts. They are to contact the person by phone or e-mail two weeks after the training to see how he or she is doing with the new learning he or she took away from the session.
6. Ask each participant to call out the name on the index card he or she holds, look at the person, and say, "I'll be in touch."

Processing the Activity
- Ask participants why this activity can be helpful to them (because it holds them accountable).
- Wish participants well and say goodbye.

Trainer/Facilitator Insights

_____

_____

_____

_____

_____

_____

_____

_____

➣ Make a Date

Purpose　This activity will help participants retain new friendships.

Risk Level　Moderate

Time　15 minutes

Number of Participants　Unlimited (small groups of six to eight)

Materials/Preparation　None

Directions

1. Tell participants that during their time in this training session they have made valuable connections with other group members. Explain that often we have the best of intentions to stay connected, but lose touch once the training is over.
2. Ask participants to make dates with other people in their groups to have phone or e-mail conversations. If participants are members of the same organization, they may want to make a lunch date.
3. Tell them to make sure to record the dates and times on their calendars. They may also want to share phone numbers and addresses.

Processing the Activity

- Offer your own business card to participants.
- Thank everyone and say goodbye.

Trainer/Facilitator Insights

_____

_____

_____

_____

_____

_____

_____

➤ About the Authors

Miriam McLaughlin is the author or co-author of numerous books, articles, and training materials. She is a freelance writer and contract trainer working as a Master Trainer for the American Lung Association and as consultant/trainer for the Yale University School Development Program. She has trained for numerous schools, businesses, and nonprofit organizations nationwide. Ms. McLaughlin resides in North Carolina.

Sandra Peyser graduated from the University of Florida and North Carolina State University. She is retired from the North Carolina Department of Public Instruction as a school counseling consultant. Ms. Peyser is the co-author of numerous training books and materials and conducts workshops for a variety of organizations. She lives in North Carolina, where she is involved in volunteer community projects.

➤ How to Use the CD

System Requirements

PC with Microsoft Windows 2003 or later
Mac with Apple OS version 10.1 or later

Using the CD With Windows

To view the items located on the CD, follow these steps:

1. Insert the CD into your computer's CD-ROM drive.

2. A window appears with the following options:

   Contents: Allows you to view the files included on the CD.
   Software: Allows you to install useful software from the CD.
   Links: Displays a hyperlinked page of websites.
   Author: Displays a page with information about the author(s).
   Contact Us: Displays a page with information on contacting the publisher or author.
   Help: Displays a page with information on using the CD.
   Exit: Closes the interface window.

If you do not have autorun enabled, or if the autorun window does not appear, follow these steps to access the CD:

1. Click Start → Run.

2. In the dialog box that appears, type d:\start.exe, where d is the letter of your CD-ROM drive. This brings up the autorun window described in the preceding set of steps.

3. Choose the desired option from the menu. (See Step 2 in the preceding list for a description of these options.)

In Case of Trouble

If you experience difficulty using the CD, please follow these steps:

1. Make sure your hardware and systems configurations conform to the systems requirements noted under "System Requirements" above.

2. Review the installation procedure for your type of hardware and operating system. It is possible to reinstall the software if necessary.

To speak with someone in Product Technical Support, call 800-762-2974 or 317-572-3994 Monday through Friday from 8:30 A.M. to 5:00 P.M. EST. You can also contact Product Technical Support and get support information through our website at www.wiley.com/techsupport.

Before calling or writing, please have the following information available:

- Type of computer and operating system.

- Any error messages displayed.

- Complete description of the problem.

It is best if you are sitting at your computer when making the call.

Pfeiffer Publications Guide

This guide is designed to familiarize you with the various types of Pfeiffer publications. The formats section describes the various types of products that we publish; the methodologies section describes the many different ways that content might be provided within a product. We also provide a list of the topic areas in which we publish.

FORMATS

In addition to its extensive book-publishing program, Pfeiffer offers content in an array of formats, from fieldbooks for the practitioner to complete, ready-to-use training packages that support group learning.

FIELDBOOK Designed to provide information and guidance to practitioners in the midst of action. Most fieldbooks are companions to another, sometimes earlier, work, from which its ideas are derived; the fieldbook makes practical what was theoretical in the original text. Fieldbooks can certainly be read from cover to cover. More likely, though, you'll find yourself bouncing around following a particular theme, or dipping in as the mood, and the situation, dictate.

HANDBOOK A contributed volume of work on a single topic, comprising an eclectic mix of ideas, case studies, and best practices sourced by practitioners and experts in the field.

An editor or team of editors usually is appointed to seek out contributors and to evaluate content for relevance to the topic. Think of a handbook not as a ready-to-eat meal, but as a cookbook of ingredients that enables you to create the most fitting experience for the occasion.

RESOURCE Materials designed to support group learning. They come in many forms: a complete, ready-to-use exercise (such as a game); a comprehensive resource on one topic (such as conflict management) containing a variety of methods and approaches; or a collection of like-minded activities (such as icebreakers) on multiple subjects and situations.

TRAINING PACKAGE An entire, ready-to-use learning program that focuses on a particular topic or skill. All packages comprise a guide for the facilitator/trainer and a workbook for the participants. Some packages are supported with additional media—such as video—or learning aids, instruments, or other devices to help participants understand concepts or practice and develop skills.

- *Facilitator/trainer's guide* Contains an introduction to the program, advice on how to organize and facilitate the learning event, and step-by-step instructor notes. The guide also contains copies of presentation materials—handouts, presentations, and overhead designs, for example—used in the program.

- *Participant's workbook* Contains exercises and reading materials that support the learning goal and serves as a valuable reference and support guide for participants in the weeks and months that follow the learning event. Typically, each participant will require his or her own workbook.

ELECTRONIC CD-ROMs and web-based products transform static Pfeiffer content into dynamic, interactive experiences. Designed to take advantage of the searchability, automation, and ease-of-use that technology provides, our e-products bring convenience and immediate accessibility to your workspace.

METHODOLOGIES

CASE STUDY A presentation, in narrative form, of an actual event that has occurred inside an organization. Case studies are not prescriptive, nor are they used to prove a point; they are designed to develop critical analysis and decision-making skills. A case study has a specific time frame, specifies a sequence of events, is narrative in structure, and contains a plot structure—an issue (what should be/have been done?). Use case studies when the goal is to enable participants to apply previously learned theories to the circumstances in the case, decide what is pertinent, identify the real issues, decide what should have been done, and develop a plan of action.

ENERGIZER A short activity that develops readiness for the next session or learning event. Energizers are most commonly used after a break or lunch to stimulate or refocus the group. Many involve some form of physical activity, so they are a useful way to counter post-lunch lethargy. Other uses include transitioning from one topic to another, where "mental" distancing is important.

EXPERIENTIAL LEARNING ACTIVITY (ELA) A facilitator-led intervention that moves participants through the learning cycle from experience to application (also known as a Structured Experience). ELAs are carefully thought-out designs in which there is a definite learning purpose and intended outcome. Each step—everything that participants do during the activity—facilitates the accomplishment of the stated goal. Each ELA includes complete instructions for facilitating the intervention and a clear statement of goals, suggested group size and timing, materials required, an explanation of the process, and, where appropriate, possible variations to the activity. (For more detail on Experiential Learning Activities, see the Introduction to the *Reference Guide to Handbooks and Annuals*, 1999 edition, Pfeiffer, San Francisco.)

GAME A group activity that has the purpose of fostering team spirit and togetherness in addition to the achievement of a pre-stated goal. Usually contrived—undertaking a desert expedition, for example—this type of learning method offers an engaging means for participants to demonstrate and practice business and interpersonal skills. Games are effective for team building and personal development mainly because the goal is subordinate to the process—the means through which participants reach decisions, collaborate, communicate, and generate trust and understanding. Games often engage teams in "friendly" competition.

ICEBREAKER A (usually) short activity designed to help participants overcome initial anxiety in a training session and/or to acquaint the participants with one another. An icebreaker can be a fun activity or can be tied to specific topics or training goals. While a useful tool in itself, the icebreaker comes into its own in situations where tension or resistance exists within a group.

INSTRUMENT A device used to assess, appraise, evaluate, describe, classify, and summarize various aspects of human behavior. The term used to describe an instrument depends primarily on its format and purpose. These terms include survey, questionnaire, inventory, diagnostic, survey, and poll. Some uses of instruments include providing instrumental feedback to group members, studying here-and-now processes or functioning within a group, manipulating group composition, and evaluating outcomes of training and other interventions.

Instruments are popular in the training and HR field because, in general, more growth can occur if an individual is provided with a method for focusing specifically on his or her own behavior. Instruments also are used to obtain information that will serve as a basis for change and to assist in workforce planning efforts.

Paper-and-pencil tests still dominate the instrument landscape with a typical package comprising a facilitator's guide, which offers advice on administering the instrument and interpreting the collected data, and an initial set of instruments. Additional instruments are available separately. Pfeiffer, though, is investing heavily in e-instruments. Electronic instrumentation provides effortless distribution and, for larger groups particularly, offers advantages over paper-and-pencil tests in the time it takes to analyze data and provide feedback.

LECTURETTE A short talk that provides an explanation of a principle, model, or process that is pertinent to the participants' current learning needs. A lecturette is intended to establish a common language bond between the trainer and the participants by providing a mutual frame of reference. Use a lecturette as an introduction to a group activity or event, as an interjection during an event, or as a handout.

MODEL A graphic depiction of a system or process and the relationship among its elements. Models provide a frame of reference and something more tangible, and more easily remembered, than a verbal explanation. They also give participants something to "go on," enabling them to track their own progress as they experience the dynamics, processes, and relationships being depicted in the model.

ROLE PLAY A technique in which people assume a role in a situation/scenario: a customer service rep in an angry-customer exchange, for example. The way in which the role is approached is then discussed and feedback is offered. The role play is often repeated using a different approach and/or incorporating changes made based on feedback received. In other words, role playing is a spontaneous interaction involving realistic behavior under artificial (and safe) conditions.

SIMULATION A methodology for understanding the interrelationships among components of a system or process. Simulations differ from games in that they test or use a model that depicts or mirrors some aspect of reality in form, if not necessarily in content. Learning occurs by studying the effects of change on one or more factors of the model. Simulations are commonly used to test hypotheses about what happens in a system—often referred to as "what if?" analysis—or to examine best-case/worst-case scenarios.

THEORY A presentation of an idea from a conjectural perspective. Theories are useful because they encourage us to examine behavior and phenomena through a different lens.

TOPICS

The twin goals of providing effective and practical solutions for workforce training and organization development and meeting the educational needs of training and human resource professionals shape Pfeiffer's publishing program. Core topics include the following:

Leadership & Management

Communication & Presentation

Coaching & Mentoring

Training & Development

E-Learning

Teams & Collaboration

OD & Strategic Planning

Human Resources

Consulting

Discover more at Pfeiffer.com

- The best in workplace performance solutions for training and HR professionals

- Online assessments

- Custom training solutions

- Downloadable training tools, exercises, and content

- Training tips, articles, and news

- Author guidelines, information on becoming a Pfeiffer Partner, and much more

Discover more at www.pfeiffer.com

Lightning Source UK Ltd.
Milton Keynes UK
UKHW021922200120
357294UK00007B/437